Loving You,
Thinking of You,
Don't Forget
to Pray

Loving You, Thinking of You, Don't Forget to Pray

LETTERS TO MY SON IN PRISON

JACQUELINE L. JACKSON

INTRODUCTION BY
CONGRESSMAN JESSE L. JACKSON, JR.

Arcade Publishing • New York

First Edition

The author has made every effort to ensure that the information within this
book was correct at the time of publication. Some letters have been redacted
for privacy, sensitivity, and discretion or to preserve the intended context of the
subject matter.

Mrs. Jackson's and Congressman Jackson's trademarks are their property
respectively and may not be used without licensing permission from the owner.

Arcade Publishing books may be purchased in bulk at special discounts for
sales promotion, corporate gifts, fund-raising, or educational purposes. Special
editions can also be created to specifications. For details, contact the Special
Sales Department, Arcade Publishing, 307 West 36th Street, 11th Floor,
New York, NY 10018 or arcade@skyhorsepublishing.com.

Arcade Publishing® is a registered trademark of Skyhorse Publishing, Inc.®,
a Delaware corporation.

Visit our website at www.arcadepub.com.

10 9 8 7 6 5 4 3 2 1

Library of Congress Cataloging-in-Publication Data is available on file.
Library of Congress Cataloging-in-Publication Control Number: 2018043369

Cover design by Brian Peterson
Cover photograph: Jacqueline L. Jackson

ISBN: 9781948924320
Ebook ISBN: 9781948924337

Printed in the United States of America

Contents

Special Tribute from Congressman Jackson

To the God of Abraham, Ishmael, Isaac, Jacob, David,
and Jesus of Nazareth who blessed me with
My Mother
who taught me at an early age to pray, and convinced me
I am never alone. I love you!

In Loving Memory of My Grandmothers:
Gertrude Brown
and
Helen Burns Jackson

To My Father, My Daughter, My Son, and
the 68 Million Men, Women, and Families who have endured
incarceration and the American Journey.
Loving You Always, Thinking of You, Don't Forget to Pray.

CONGRESSMAN JESSE L. JACKSON, JR.

Preface

May 28, 2013

Judge Amy Berman Jackson
US District Court
For the District of Columbia

Dear Judge Amy Berman Jackson,

I am Jacqueline Jackson, the mother of five children, one of whom I am writing about, my son Jesse Jackson, Jr. As my son stood before you in your courtroom, in a state of contrition, I wish to thank you for allowing him the time he needed to gain his composure. Your patience also helped my family to endure an extremely difficult family ordeal.

Judge Amy Berman Jackson, as I struggle to compose the words that may help to shape a better understanding of who my son is and to share with you a little about his background, my heart is in a great deal of pain. I am hurting not just for what could be my son's fate. I am hurting not for my family alone. But I feel the weight of millions of mothers and family members who lack the courage, or the opportunity, or the ability, to pen their emotions regarding our justice system. I believe there should be nonviolent solutions and remedies for nonviolent crimes that do not require the violence of totally removing a person from his or her community.

I feel compelled to seize this moment to ask that you consider a new approach for handling nonviolent offenses. This letter is an appeal for not just my son, but for the chance we may have to construct a more enlightened system of justice—one that is more applicable and appropriate for the twenty-first century. If our national goal is to create a more civil society, should not we seek tools and techniques that attempt to develop men and women into productive contributors to society? Could not the goal of a just and civil society most likely be achieved by a restorative justice system that has as its principles compassion and reparative justice? Restorative justice is an approach to justice or fairness that focuses on the needs of the victims and the offenders, as well as the involved community, instead of satisfying abstract legal principles or just punishing the offenders. Restorative justice is more inclined toward restitution, providing altruistic services within the community affected, and monitoring the behavior of the offender.

Let there be no mistake: all who know me know I subscribe to my mother's law, "There is only one way and that's the right way." I believe completely in reward, punishment, mercy, and redemption. But if there is honest contrition and remorse for a nonviolent crime, restorative justice is a system that exhibits compassion. It also offers a greater guarantee for restored behavior than the punishment-based system with its high level of recidivism. I urge you to view this matter and the fate of my son within the larger context of how the United States compares with the global society and how America treats men and women who are found guilty of nonviolent crimes. When I realized that the United States has 4.4 percent of the total world population but, by some estimates, 22 percent of the prisoners of the world, I understood that this stark reality creates the need for new solutions. I feel our justice system would be well served by such an exemplary decision.

Your Honor, Judge Amy Berman Jackson, my husband was granted a Rockefeller Scholarship to attend Chicago Theological Seminary. With a family of almost three in 1964, we arrived at McGifford House on Woodlawn Avenue in Chicago. By the time my son was born, my husband was attending school and organizing the Kenwood Oakland Community Organization (KOCO) and was its first executive director (an unsalaried position). Because of the success of this organization, and based on the recommendation of Rev. James Bevel, my husband was hired to work for the Southern Christian Leadership Conference for $75. If my memory serves me correctly, that was his weekly salary. To sustain our family, we were given food baskets by our Pastor, Rev. Clay Evans, and his members of Fellowship Missionary Baptist Church, where my son Jesse Jr. chose later to be baptized. I learned to provide the other necessities by frequenting resale shops, lawn sales, learning to preserve and can foods, and sewing and mending things that did not fit. But most of all, I learned to express my appreciation and gratitude for the kindness of others.

Contrary to the belief of many who only see us as we are today from a televised perspective, Jesse Jr. was not born with a silver spoon nor was he born privileged. Jesse Jr., my second child and my eldest son, was born during the turbulent sixties, the period of terrible hatred for Dr. Martin Luther King Jr. and those who followed

Dr. King and the principles of nonviolence he espoused. Our son, Rev. Jackson's namesake, inherited his friends and enemies. As a child, Jesse Jr. held jobs waiting tables, cleaning floors, and other odd jobs. Growing up in the shadow of his father, Jesse Jr. has always tried desperately to live up to the expectations we have had for him. I think perhaps he has tried too hard.

I recall how disappointed Jesse Jr. was when he discovered he could not enter high school without repeating the ninth grade. My husband finally convinced him to accept this as his challenge. Rev. Jackson said, "Sometimes you must go down to come up," and Jesse Jr. prevailed. He completed his undergraduate studies in three years, received a juris doctor degree, and received his master's degree in theology. His passion for the Word of God led me to believe and hope he would find his niche in theology. However, he chose public service, the United States Congress, and we are proud of his choice and the good he accomplished during his seventeen years of perfect attendance and sterling voting record. I suppose the true testimony of my son's service was demonstrated by his constituency when he was unable to serve them. The wonderful people of the 2nd Congressional District showed their appreciation, loyalty, and support by reelecting him.

I received a call from my daughter Santita, who requested that I check on Jesse Jr. because she was concerned for him sometime during the last weeks of June 2012. I did as she requested and found my son grossly underweight and in poor health. He asked that I take him to the office because he had an upcoming vote. When I took him to his Capitol Hill office to prepare for the vote, the office was in total disarray, which was most unusual for my son. A security guard approached me and said, "Please take care of Jesse. Last week he collapsed on the floor of the House and was taken to the hospital by ambulance." My heart sank. No one had shared with me my son's condition. I called my husband. We told our son to "Come with us.

We are going to get help for you." He did not offer any resistance, which made us know his condition was dire. Everything that has happened since that day is public record. My son is much better now.

My mother says, "There is always some good in all things." There was a transforming moment during the horrific trial experience. As my son Jesse Jr. faced the judge, he turned around to look for his father's support just as he did when he had to repeat the ninth grade. His lips shaped the words, "I love you, and I am so sorry." I shall never forget that moment because my heart leapt. I then realized the joy and love that sustains all mothers. I love my son. May God guide your decision.

Yours truly,
Mrs. Jesse L. Jackson, Sr.

Acknowledgments

This book could not be possible without the God Factor. This expression was given to me by the late Dr. Lamont Godwin as I spoke to him about a problem for which I was not optimistic about the result. He said, "Mrs. J, always leave room for the God Factor." That was about twenty years ago, and it has worked for me. What is the God Factor? It is leaving room for God to manage the outcome in all of life's situations. Leave room for God in your plans. That has worked for me.

I want to thank my husband of 56 years, Reverend Jesse Jackson, Sr., for his kindness and his patience.

I thank my children, Santita, Jesse, Jonathan, Yusef, and Dr. Jacqueline. When I call their names, I smile inside. To my grand-children: may God keep you strong.

I thank my mother, who believed in God and taught me to believe. Her belief encouraged me to become the bearer of high expectations.

My mother has always loved her first-born grandson, Jesse Jr., who always had his way with her. Even though he advanced and matured, with him she remained childlike. On every trip, whether it was a vacation or convention, my mother insisted on sharing a room with the boys. And they hated it. She, at the end of the day, would unfailingly become the subject of every disagreement among them. Oh, how we miss her energy!

I would like to thank my three sisters, Mrs. Constance Ward, Dr. Maurice McNeil, and Ms. Betty Magness.

When my son told me he wanted to publish some of the letters, I hesitated. Then, after a few days, I reluctantly capitulated because the letters were not mine. To him, they belonged.

What began as a Mother's Day gift of privately printed letters to my son blossomed into a peek into the life of a mother who longed for her child.

There are so many I must thank for their devotion to the completion of this project. Ms. April L. Smith and Ms. Nicole S. Jones saw this project through from beginning to end. They understood the intrinsic value in sharing this intimate gesture of connection and communication between a mother and a son with the public. They supported the macrocosmic nature of human support and love embedded in the letters. They pushed me all the way.

To my son's childhood friends who reached out to support him, I thank you. I am grateful to Attorney C. K. Hoffler and to Attorney Judy Smith and especially to Alanna Ford for collecting all of the letters that were written. I will be eternally grateful to the late Don Harris, who meticulously managed the Congressman's property and who wrote letters daily. I thank my friend Mrs. Juanita Passmore, who took her letter writing seriously. Mrs. Passmore made certain every word was perfect, heartfelt, and of God.

To my friends Mr. Corry and Dara, who took turns driving me back and forth from Washington, DC to Butner, North Carolina's Federal Penal Institution: Thank you. We would start out from Washington at 4 a.m. to make it to the facility by 8 a.m., when the doors open. Mr. Corry, who drove me most often, committed to an even greater sacrifice to the extent that he waited outside the facility for the duration of my visit. His only reward, after a quick stop at the nearby Cracker Barrel, was my spirited conversation about all that I had just experienced. For his friendship and dutifulness, I am most grateful.

To the anonymous family who generously shared their quarters with me because I did not know to bring quarters for the vending machine that provided the snacks for our hours-long visit, thank you for your spontaneous kindness.

To those incarcerated as then-residents of Butner Federal Penal Institution who are members of the Nation of Islam and thereby assured me they would look after and counsel my son: May God continue to bless your work within and outside the correctional institution.

To Sister Claudette, also a member of the Nation of Islam, thank you for your dedication in ensuring that my son received a copy of the *Final Call* newspaper.

To the Calhouns for their multipronged commitment, as they not only provided me with transportation but guidance and hospitality. They would first assist me by picking me up—at times, in Atlanta, then driving me to my hotel in Alabama—even providing me with vending machine quarters. They also took the care to help me navigate entry into the Montgomery Federal Prison Camp into which my son had been transferred. The Calhouns found and provided me with the logistical information necessary to reach the prison via a designated busing system. They transported me to the bus stop by 7 a.m., showed me where to stand in line, and then they too waited hours after my departure for me to visit and return from the prison. They offered me friendship, companionship, and clarity in a daunting endeavor to maintain a connection with my son. For their patience, time, and commitment I am immeasurably thankful.

There is a wide net of constituents of the Second Congressional District of Illinois who supported my son and his family during the highs and the lows. My love and gratitude for them cannot be measured. To the Chicagoans! Thank you for that "Getting Up Spirit." We are the champions!

For the countless pastors who lent their faith to our family; for my pastor, Reverend Clay Evans; and for my church family, The Fellowship Missionary Baptist Church, who prayed for my family for the duration of my son's thirty-month period of incarceration, I am grateful. Thank you.

To those who wrote letters of character reference for my son: You shared with me how he impacted your lives and his love for his job.

Finally, my son turned this seemingly rainy period into a second act. Ironically, I taught him to ride the waves, and now he teaches me to surf. Thank you, my son.

Introduction

It was a difficult decision for me to arrive at the publication of these letters. On the one hand, they are so immensely personal; on the other, I thought it important to balance the struggles of the desires of men I met in prison, who served far longer than I had, and had never received a single letter.

It is sad to say that most people do not die from biological illnesses or even heart attacks. Most people die from abandonment. However, they still walk, and they still breathe.

In prison, I observed men who were experiencing, and had experienced, abandonment. They indeed were the Walking Dead.

Just after the four o'clock count in federal prison, every inmate would wait anxiously to hear the names called. "Mail call, mail call," the prison guard would shout. He would then proceed to call out each piece of mail and the inmate recipient.

I would watch men rush to mail call, only to see their heads drop when their names were not called. There I would stand, and on some days, my name would be called ten times. I would look around and see in the eyes of other men both disdain and envy. There were even times that I would let other men share in the reading of my letters, magazines, and periodicals. That they might glean some hope, and even feel as though they were part of a family, and not abandoned.

The letters from my mother provided that comfort while I was incarcerated. She made a promise to me, which I did not expect her to keep. In fact, I was hoping she would not keep it. I wanted to be left alone, and I truthfully did not care if I were forgotten about. I wanted to be out of the media, out of the public eye, even out of my family's eye. My mother, however, was not going to let that happen.

There is a tremendous amount of shame, blame, and guilt in the life of every person. Some have more shame than blame and guilt, others have more blame than guilt and shame, still others have more guilt than shame and blame. SBG exists in every human life, in some shape or form. It is simply there. It is part of what it means to be human. Rarely, however, do people recognize the SBG in their life.

SBG is the dominant characteristic among the inmate population. I never met a single man in prison who did anything wrong— at least that's the story they would tell. Blaming someone else and not accepting responsibility for their behavior, no matter how small the part they played, was also a dominant characteristic. Not wanting their children or family members to even know they were in jail is certainly the shame factor. But it is that guilt thing, that self-debilitating mental condition where a man has to sleep with himself at night, knowing the truth of that which has been privately on display, and in my case publicly.

My mother would tell me to forgive myself. I observed other men who, not having come to terms with their own guilt, had not even reached the phase of self-forgiveness; they were in denial. I learned a lot about myself from them. I learned that I needed to accept responsibility, and in doing so I sought to encourage others to accept responsibility for their behavior in prison.

Prison is lonely. Being removed from people that you love, from your neighbors, for any extended period of time, is extremely difficult. I met men in prison who had never seen a cell phone or laptop.

Time stands still in their lives, however, the cycle of their offense that landed them in the joint is tied to the shame and the blame and the guilt, and the constant replaying, reminiscing of the events in their lives that landed them in the camp or behind the fence.

My mother's letters came as a soothing light of daybreak to the darkness of the stark reality of confinement. When I first read the letters, I needed them to hold on. After my release, I began rereading the letters for perspective.

Incarcerated men need both hope and perspective.

The hope is as basic as the occasional letter. The hope also comes from rehabilitation, because there is the expectation that one will turn from their wicked ways by accepting responsibility, leaving prison, and writing a very different narrative that includes the forward motion of the true self.

Perspective is equally important. There are 68 million of us. We've been through this process with minimal hope of public forgiveness for our very publicly documented behavior. The idea that a man or woman can do what the judge says do, can do what the jury says do, and can even accept responsibility for the behavior but remain a felon for the rest of his or her life, must ultimately be seen by the American people as punishment on top of punishment.

While in prison, I hoped not only to endure incarceration but to persevere and endure the life of a felon.

As I served time, the hope of the touch and the feel of someone from the outside world who is thinking of you was important. My perspective was firm that, as a felon, the rest of my life would be on eggshells, even for something as basic as a traffic stop.

For more than fifty years, my mother has been the matriarch of our family. Just about everyone knows the patriarch. But the matriarch made choices. These letters not only provided me hope, but upon closer reflection, I see the pain and the cathartic and therapeutic representations in my mother's own words that only a mother could feel.

Loving you . . . Thinking of you . . . Don't forget to pray. This symphony of words soothed and sustained me on days when nothing else could or would during the dank, murky midnights of my life. Sometimes I questioned God. But I never questioned my mother. Only Mom's love could resonate through these most harrowing and turbulent times of my life. I read her letters every day; every night; every afternoon. I cherished them. These tender words were my mother's words in my mother's pen. She wrote me every single day while I was imprisoned.

Every.

Single.

Day.

Mom's letters were never interrupted. They always came. I could smell her perfume and what she cooked that day. I could count on them. I could plan my day around them. Sometimes I would receive three letters in one day. How I loved those days. How I love my mom.

I am honored to share this gift of Mom's letters with you. . . . This is a journey of immeasurable, boundless love.

I am the product of great expectations. When I fell short, my mother, my first love, the beautiful Mrs. Jacqueline Lavinia Jackson, made me believe I still had hope and could still dream impossible dreams, even when it seemed mighty grim. My fall from grace was a long one, or so I thought. Mom instilled her truths, God's truths, in me every day . . . every single day. It is as if she provided me with a road map to navigate my darkest days of solitude. She was determined.

And even when I did not respond, Mom still wrote. She never gave up. My letters still came. She made a promise and she kept it. "I will write you every day, Son."

Briefly, I mulled over sharing these very personal letters with you, but something kept tugging at me. I know and wholeheartedly believe that Mom's letters shall garner the universal appeal they deserve. My wish is, as they have empowered me, they may edify and uplift others. This tome will give others a real glimpse of how a mother's love, my mother's love, truly transforms.

I learned a great deal more about Mom during my confinement, and I treasure her even more for making the conscious choice to pour out her heart and for selflessly sharing all the daily aspects of her life with me. It required great discipline and great love—Mom was busy.

Ashamedly, I never stopped to ask my mother how she was daily when I was at the height of my success, yet during my restraint, I learned to reacquaint our love. My mother compelled me to fall even deeper into enlightenment and into God's great counsel through her letters. And I learned to understand Mom even more. These letters were, for me, the Holy Grail; the Great Manifesto. How Mom rebuilt me through these letters. And I thought I knew everything about my mother. Mom is tough, but oh so very tender. I have the letters. Please do not share this secret.

Mom caused me to remember my truest self. She made me recall the two M&Ms (Morals & Manners). She made me taste our glorious holiday meals. She made me see life in color again. She put hope in my brain.

Although Mom is known all over the world as a civil, human, and women's rights activist, and devoted wife of civil rights icon, the Reverend Jesse Jackson, Sr., she prides herself on being a mother and being in the business of raising her children. She says there is no better contribution to the world. I did not understand this position until I decided to "not lean unto my own understanding." I too realized that while Mom seems diminutive in size, she is a powerhouse of wisdom, scripture, folklore, knowledge, culture, fortitude, tenacity, influence, zeal, grace, and mercy and fun, so much fun. The times were too many to count when her letters made me roar with laughter.

Mom always fascinated me because there seemed to be nothing

she could not do. Her strength could match any Goliath. And Mom always wins. She informed me about her knitting and cooking, caring for her own mother and her mother-in-law (my grandmothers—my other two favorites), and all things Jackson. There were even some details she told me not to share, as my mother loves a good and juicy story. I loved those letters.

I share these letters with you from a mother who made me believe she loved me and showed that she loved me unconditionally. She did not judge. She was not boastful. She did not send one "I told you so letter," which surprised even me. She sent pure unadulterated love, and I felt it leap out of her heart onto the pages, laser-pointed directly to me. How these letters made me crave her embrace. I craved her laughter. I craved her Southern charm. I craved her cooking and her sternness. I craved her guidance. I craved her steadying thread.

Mom shared with me about her deep love for my father and her devotion to their vows and their mission together but also to her children. She is family first. I have profound respect for Mom for providing the foundation and being serious about it. It's her life's work and her legacy. Mom shared glimpses of her growing up with strict rules in Fort Pierce, Florida. She shared with me the predicaments of the world and those we still need to solve. Mom even asked for my opinion. Imagine that. She engaged my love of discourse.

And her visits were legendary. But her letters . . . you will see.

I share with you my most precious gifts . . . the thoughts and dreams of my mom who once said, "We must embrace our children not to be led to believe they are less than who they are."

I am whole again because of Mom's love and endless letters. I am set free.

And she told me she was proud of me.

And I believed Mom. God makes no mistakes. Allow me to introduce you to Mom.

How I love her.
How I love these letters.
And of course, her chitterlings. Glory be to God.

Sincerely,
32453–016

Loving You,
Thinking of You,
Don't Forget
to Pray

Prologue

My son asked me a question: "Why did you write me every day?"

MY RESPONSE TO HIM:

1. I didn't want you to lose hope. Hope is contagious. So, when you have it, you can share it with others.

2. I did not want you to feel abandoned and lonely.

3. I know one cannot help someone else without helping themselves, so writing to you was therapy for me, and it helped to ease my pain.

4. I wanted you to remain informed daily of the sounds of home.

5. I wanted all those around you to know that you are very loved.

THINKING OF YOU

My Son,

I love you and wish I could have been with you on Monday. I am stronger than you think. I want you to "be strong and of good courage." Don't forget to read the Bible. I am going to send you one. Do it as often as you can. I didn't read my assignment today . . . was too tired. I will get back to my reading tomorrow.

Remember, all life has purpose and meaning, and only God directs the meaningful purpose, not friends or family. The approval from others is often misguided and will lead you down the wrong path.

I found this stationery in the basement. I used it as an invitation during the '70s for an EXPO event, and now I am using it for you. Will write more.

Love you,
Mom

THINKING OF YOU

My Son,

I couldn't go out today. The media has me confined to the house. I avoided having the people who are working on the house here today, didn't want them subjected to the press.

Tomorrow is always a better day. I am very, very proud of you, Jesse, and I thank you for your service to so many.

James came over to help carve a path, so I can move around all this clutter. Yusef recommended I leave my ceiling open for 6 months, so I can find the exterior water that's coming into the house. I agreed so the next owner won't have this problem.

Today I read from pages 353–403. This portion is very good; got lost in several chapters before. Some of this appears hesitantly created, and is not in the same voice.

You are a very scholarly writer; we will continue to work on this. The conclusion and your writing make this a great story. This document is very sensitive and needs some corrections, and should include LeMans, St. Albans, and Jim Camps picking up you and friends, and because he had been drinking, you all were left on the side of the road without any means of communication with adults to pick you up. You decided to be the one to walk miles to find a phone.

Eddie Bow stopped by today . . . stayed most of the day to show his support.

You were the story of the day. One commentator said you tried to break into jail, something he had not seen before.

The newspaper gave to the public your address and ID number, so the people could write you negative letters.

At this time, only read the letters from people you recognize and save all the letters you receive for the future, please.

I love you,
Mom

THINKING OF YOU

My Son,

I have decided to write to you every day you are away from me and to pray the Prayers of David.

I heard from lawyer CK this morning. She said you are doing well. News I am happy to hear. The pictures of you on TV are very flattering. CK did well recalling the day's events.

I called attorney Paul Langer to negotiate with the insurance company. I am going to let the insurance contractors go and do this work with someone else. I am not pleased with these guys, but I am okay with this because I worked on the house in Washington and gained a lot of experience.

Today, almost simultaneously, Yusef texted asking me to convince my mom to come to Chicago on Thursday. Mr. Corry texted me to tell me he is in NC, 80 miles from you, at his niece's house. He also has some family who works there. How small is the world?

It rained cats and dogs this evening. I am getting ready for Halloween. Will send you some pictures of the children in costumes. I love you.

October 31, 2013

LOVING YOU

Dear Son,

It is Halloween, and the forecast is rain all day and late into the night. Normally, we have a little parade for the children and their parents in our community to show off their costumes. If I dress in time, I'll participate; it's really a big fun experience.

I asked some of the "important people in charge" to cancel the neighborhood parade due to the rain. Those mean asses—you know who they are—said, "No, if you don't want to participate, just turn your lights off." That really wet my spirit.

So I passed out treats at Yusef's. Jonathan always has his lights out. I think he became angry about the enormous crowd the neighborhood attracts. This community attracts about 300 to 400 children and their parents. The children are very orderly.

Eddie Bow stayed off work to spend the day and evening with us. We also used James as security. Everything went well.

Love you,
Mom

LOVING YOU EACH DAY

My Son,

How are you? You are doing well, I hope.

Isaiah 54:17 says, "'No weapon that is formed against thee shall prosper, and every tongue that shall rise against thee in judgment thou shalt condemn. This is the heritage of the servants of the Lord and their righteousness is of me,' saith the Lord."

I am allowing you adjustment time. You must know we will be down there soon. I don't mind sitting outside the gate until they let me see you.

This morning, the *Sun-Times* announced the sale of the beer business. Nearly everyone we have ever known has been calling. This is strange. I don't know what to make of all this excitement.

They just signed the papers. These contracts can take months to be enacted.

The *Sun-Times* is always so very nasty to us. One commentator said Yusef didn't really run the company, he just passed out tickets to family and friends.

They began the article with "Yusef, the son of Jesse Jackson and the brother-in-law of the Alderman Sandi Jackson."

It made Yusef angry. I told Yusef, "Dogs don't bark at parked cars." So long as he continues to move forward, he will hear the growls.

Ms. Ford and I spent the day together. There were only a few

November 1, 2013

staff members there at the office today because of the Atlanta Conference, so we ran some PUSH errands. Will write more.

Love you,
Mom

November 2, 2013

Dear Son,

How are you? I hope you are adjusting okay. I don't know what to make of this, and I find this to be something I must deal with, but not accept.

I pray every day that God continues to protect and guide our families. Don't forget to pray. I learned the 1st Psalms while in the first grade. Please read the Psalms.

Yusef and Reverend are out of town; I took Leah and Skye to lunch at the Grand Lux. But not before I was bombarded with phone calls about Jonathan's moving presentation at PUSH, so we went to PUSH to pick up the CD.

We listened to his speech in the car. Leah, Skye, and I cried the entire speech. The speech was about his love for you. "Where is our brother?" The question God asked Cain. His reply, "Am I my brother's keeper?"

He talked about the two systems, one for you and one for J. P. Morgan. I want you to know Yusef asked that we be allowed to pay back your debt. We were told no, and yet they over-negotiated with J. P. Morgan.

We sold a lot of tapes today. Jonathan was good. You must hear the tape. It may be online.

While downtown with Leah, Marilyn called me to see if I had heard from Little Jonathan; he was 5 hours late from school. I left Macy's immediately with Leah to return to his home. This evening, he decided to hang with his friends without getting permission? I am going to spend some time with him.

There is a lot of love for you.

Our project will be perfect whenever you begin to work on it again.

Love you,
Mom

THINKING OF YOU

Dear Son,

Please read James 1.

Are you okay? The southern night sky is the prettiest sky in America I think. Have you seen it?

Do you have a window? How large is your bed and bedroom? Is your bathroom in your room, or in another location? Are you locked away at night? Do you have access to TV or radio? What do you do each day? Why haven't I heard from you?

Monday will be a week since I have heard from you. I am beginning to worry.

Today I went to see Allene. She told me to tell you "hello." And she sends her prayers and love. Eddie Bow and I went to see *12 Years a Slave*. It is a very emotional movie, and a very, very important movie for us in America and as Americans.

I am told it is not making any money. That makes me sad. I am very impressed with the courage it took to make this film. It's a great script, and the acting is excellent.

It should be in the category of *Anne Frank* and *Schindler's List*, but it may be that the experience is still too fresh in the minds of Afro-Americans because of racism. You are always in my thoughts. Going to bed. Good night.

Love you,
Mom

November 4, 2013

THINKING OF YOU

Dear Son,

I was happy to hear your voice! I told Jonathan I spoke with you. He wants you to call him; he loves you very much.

Your father is back. When you can, give him a call.

Hey, Marty just had his house redone with an architect to oversee the total construction. Now that's a big deal.

More tomorrow.

Love,
Mom

LOVING YOU

Dear Son,

Are you reading your Bible?

Read about David, who said, "I would have fainted had I not seen the Glory of God in the Land of the Living."[1] God shows His love and His glory here on earth. David is an excellent example of God's love for a sinner.

Glad to speak to you. Please call Jonathan; he is so worried about you. He loves you too much. He always reminisces about A&T now.

Spent the day at PUSH with Reverend. Then, we went directly into a meeting regarding Hazel and Richard Thomas's company. Hazel said someone is trying to take the company from them. We all will be meeting on this matter on Friday. I will tell you more on Friday. Please don't let him know I have given you this information.

Miss Ford said she has your storage papers but will not tell your dad.

I love you,
Mom

LOVING YOU

Dear Son,

We were happy to hear from you today. Jonathan's number is xxx-xxx-xxxx. Please call him soon.

I texted Jessica on November 3. She texted me back; that made me feel good. I was happy to hear from her also. What are you doing with your time?

Mrs. Passmore's husband died today. I think I told you Velma Wilson's husband died a week ago. Rev. Wilson's daughter got her law license several days ago.

There are three houses for sale on my block. Someone broke the window of the Smart Car last night, and we caught 3 men breaking in the house on the north side of Jonathan's house. Leah saw them and called me. Reverend and I went to the house, and the three grown men almost knocked us down getting away. It took the police over 30 minutes to respond to our two calls to the police. Unbelievable.

Don't forget to pray. Love you,
Mom

November 6, 2013

LOVING YOU

Dear Son,

Don't forget to pray!

I spent the day at the office clearing some of the debris. I try to give your dad a hand. You made the right decision to not permit him to go with you that Monday. Courtney called Yusef and said something about a debt? I told him I will pay it, or he can.

Rev went to Springfield at 1 o'clock today to lead convocation or open this session. He will return tomorrow.

He broke the bed flopping down on it. I have asked him repeatedly not to fall down into the bed; he never listens. James and I rebuilt the frame. Jo Bridges called. I am sending her your address. She wants to write you once a week, she said.

I was told John Johnson owned the entire block his building was on and his daughter has sold each building one at a time. Now she is renting two floors in the building across from the museum with the two lions on Michigan Avenue.

I think I told you someone broke the window on the Smart Car; coming in tonight, I found the stick they used. It appears to be a leg from a chair. I will write tomorrow.

Love you,
Mom

LOVING YOU

If my people, which are called by my name, shall humble themselves, and pray, and seek my face, and turn from their wicked ways; then will I hear from heaven, and will forgive their sin, and will heal their land.
II Chronicles 7:14 (KJV)

Dear Son,

I am not going to write the scripture for you. Please look it up. I hope you are feeling good. I am loving you more and more each day. People who see us are constantly telling us they are not happy with your fate. They send information to the office (anonymously of course) telling on others.

Santita saw Anita Beard at the co-op. Santita gave her my number; she called me to get to your address. She wants to write you. I'll give her your number Saturday. She has been very supportive of you for a long time.

Long day.

Love you,
Mom

THINKING OF YOU

Be kindly affectioned one to another with brotherly love;
in honour preferring one another; Not slothful in business; fervent
in spirit; serving the Lord; Rejoicing in hope; patient in tribulation;
continuing instant in prayer.
Romans 12:11 (KJV)

Dear Son,

First call this morning, Yusef trying to plan a trip to see you before Thanksgiving. I would like to bring you your favorite food. Can I?

Weber picked up my sofa and a chair that was damaged by water. I asked Weber to only clean it. If that doesn't work, I will have to have the sofa upholstered. The insurance company said they will reupholster the sofa only, but not the four matching chairs because the chairs didn't get wet. Nothing works smoothly. I am not happy with this insurance experience.

I went to PUSH to participate in a meeting today with Marty, Hazel Thomas, Eric, his sister, and Rev. Their company is having plenty of problems. Next Friday it will be resolved. I hope Hazel can save her company.

The newspaper said the Sheriff went to Willie Gary's house to confiscate his property yesterday . . . something about the debt he owed. This came as a surprise to us. It seems as if the hammer has been dropped on the black community.

I will keep you informed. Very tired.

Love you,
Mom

P.S. Amaya stopped by and said your wife and children are coming for Christmas.

November 9, 2013

LOVING YOU ALWAYS

Jesus saith unto him, I am the way, the truth, and the life:
no man cometh unto the Father, but by me.
John 14:6 (KJV)

Dear Son,

The baby was christened today at 3:00 p.m.

I went to PUSH this morning, saw Maddix Moore. He was back in Chicago taking care of his mom. It was good to see him.

The Urban League gave Rev their highest award tonight. I had to make a choice, so I decided to spend the remainder of the evening with Yusef, his family, and Jonathan's children. At some point things must stop for the children. This I have always known.

I am home now. It is late . . . I am very tired. Will write more tomorrow.

I will always love you,
Mom

November 10, 2013

I LOVE YOU

But God commendeth his love toward us, in that,
while we were yet sinners, Christ died for us.
Romans 5:8 (KJV)

My Son,

The media told of your first visit this morning. I hope all is well. We speak of you every day. Santita came over to the house after Rev's *Upfront* show; we talked about the Urban League dinner. I didn't go. I chose to stay at the baby's christening and the dinner afterwards.

Rev went to the Bears game today, they lost . . . sad.

Noah left the key in the door to the house, must go over to remove the key. Also, Santita and I are going to Whole Foods.

Will write more tomorrow. Happy Sunday.

Love,
Mom

P.S. I decided not to mail your letters every day so people won't become jealous.

November 11, 2013

LOVING YOU MORE EACH DAY

A good man out of the good treasure of the heart bringeth forth good things: and an evil man out of the evil treasure bringeth forth evil things.
Matthew 12:35 (KJV)

Dear Son,

I had to place the Smart Car in the shop to get the back window repaired. The thief didn't take your shoes; I don't know why. They are very nice. I think he simply went through the car and threw everything all over the driveway.

I sent the black cabinet in the living room to PUSH this morning. Rev is always making small talk about all the things in the house, but when I make a change he is uncomfortable.

Jan called me this morning to tell me about the increase in her mother's insurance. Her mother is dying, and she has left her job to care for her and her insurance has increased also. Before, her mother didn't have to pay anything . . . Now they must pay.

It snowed today, and the snow turned to ice tonight.

I pray for you each night. Be sure to read.

You are never alone.

Love always,
Mom

THINKING OF YOU

For God is not the author of confusion, but of peace,
as in all churches of the saints.
I Corinthians 14:33 (KJV)

My Dear Son,

Are things going well for you? Can you see the southern night sky?

The men are repairing my garage. They started to only patch the stucco, but when they started banging on it, the whole garage fell in. Now we are talking about rebuilding it . . . after I count my money.

Most of the day I have spent with Mrs. Passmore. I wrote you . . . she lost her husband Haymond. Mrs. Passmore is one of my oldest and closest married friends. She has been married 54 years. I learned how to be married from women like her, Helen Anglin (The Queen), Mrs. Vernon Exum, Ester Thompson, and so many others. You know them all.

To learn to be married, you must be with successfully married people. You know, birds of a feather flock together.

Rev is upstairs packing with John Mitchel; it is about 10:30 p.m. I just got in from the wake.

Went by the office, Alanna ate something that made her break out, I think she is getting over it now.

Don't forget to pray.

With my heart I love you,
Mom

THINKING OF YOU

Dear Son,

Psalms 23

This has been a long but very uplifting day.

Mrs. Passmore's husband's funeral was today. He was 91 years old. They have been married 61 years. Wow! How great is that? Pam, of course, was in charge as always.

I left home at about 11:15 with the assurance, based on experience, that the funeral would not begin on time and parking would not be a problem. I was scheduled to speak, without my permission. You know how I hate public speaking.

Surprise! There was not a parking space to be found for blocks. I finally found a space about 4 blocks away from the church. As soon as I walked in, it was my turn to speak. I am sure I fell on my face, but the people are always so very nice to me. Thanks be to GOD!

The pastor preached from Psalms 23, and he spent at least 6 minutes on "The Lord is my Shepherd" and no time on "He maketh me to lie down."[1]

I feel if the Lord maketh you to lie down, he had to knock you down. But you land on green pastures.

Afterward, there was dinner at Hard Times with Hermene, Sally Townsend, etc.

Then, we went to 50th on the lake and spent the rest of the evening with Hermene and Alderman Beavers. Beavers and I saw Emil Jones in the crowd.

Many of us sit on different sides of the political table, but here we talk. Sometimes, Ald. Beavers picks up my tab, and I am always grateful.

That was my day.

I love you,
Mom

A Psalm of David

The Lord is my shepherd; I shall not want.

He maketh me to lie down in green pastures: he leadeth me beside the still waters.

He restoreth my soul: he leadeth me in the paths of righteousness for his name's sake.

Yea, though I walk through the valley of the shadow of death, I will fear no evil: for thou art with me; thy rod and thy staff they comfort me.

Thou preparest a table before me in the presence of mine enemies: thou anointest my head with oil; my cup runneth over.

Surely goodness and mercy shall follow me all the days of my life: and I will dwell in the house of the Lord for ever.

Psalms 23 (KJV)

THINKING OF YOU

My Son,

How are you?

It is about one o'clock. I am off to a late start. Got my Smart Car back with the window repaired. My garage is coming along nicely.

Going to Allene's to take my mail. Then I will return home.

Nothing important today.

Love,
Mom

THINKING OF YOU

Dear Son,

Psalms 37

You are always on my mind. How are you?

Allene called me this morning to tell me she found one of my unmailed letters in a bag of mail.

I gave my mail to Santita before I went to Washington over a month ago. She said she would mail my letter and give the remaining mail to Allene to process, but instead she gave me the same mail several days ago. I don't understand her at all.

Please let me know the dates on the mail, so I will know how long she held it.

Mrs. Ford went to a conference in DC with Rainbow.

Went by PUSH today . . . slow day. People are very concerned about the health care issue. We signed people up for the program; we don't get many people participating.

What is it like where you are? When may I come see you? I want to know you are alright!

Love you too much,

Mom

A Psalm of David

Fret not thyself because of evildoers, neither be thou envious against the workers of iniquity.

For they shall soon be cut down like the grass, and wither as the green herb.

Trust in the Lord, and do good; so shalt thou dwell in the land, and verily thou shalt be fed.

Delight thyself also in the Lord; and he shall give thee the desires of thine heart.

Commit thy way unto the Lord; trust also in him; and he shall bring it to pass.

And he shall bring forth thy righteousness as the light, and thy judgment as the noonday.

Rest in the Lord, and wait patiently for him: fret not thyself because of him who prospereth in his way, because of the man who bringeth wicked devices to pass.

Cease from anger, and forsake wrath: fret not thyself in any wise to do evil.

For evildoers shall be cut off: but those that wait upon the Lord, they shall inherit the earth.

For yet a little while, and the wicked shall not be: yea, thou shalt diligently consider his place, and it shall not be.

But the meek shall inherit the earth; and shall delight themselves in the abundance of peace.

The wicked plotteth against the just, and gnasheth upon him with his teeth.

The Lord shall laugh at him: for he seeth that his day is coming.

The wicked have drawn out the sword, and have bent their bow, to cast down the poor and needy, and to slay such as be of upright conversation.

Their sword shall enter into their own heart, and their bows shall be broken.

A little that a righteous man hath is better than the riches of many wicked.

For the arms of the wicked shall be broken: but the Lord upholdeth the righteous.

The Lord knoweth the days of the upright: and their inheritance shall be forever.

They shall not be ashamed in the evil time: and in the days of famine they shall be satisfied.

But the wicked shall perish, and the enemies of the Lord shall be as the fat of lambs: they shall consume; into smoke shall they consume away.

The wicked borroweth, and payeth not again: but the righteous sheweth mercy, and giveth.

For such as be blessed of him shall inherit the earth; and they that be cursed of him shall be cut off.

The steps of a good man are ordered by the Lord: and he delighteth in his way.

Though he fall, he shall not be utterly cast down: for the Lord upholdeth him with his hand.

I have been young, and now am old; yet have I not seen the righteous forsaken, nor his seed begging bread.

He is ever merciful, and lendeth; and his seed is blessed. Depart from evil, and do good; and dwell for evermore.

For the Lord loveth judgment, and forsaketh not his saints; they are preserved forever: but the seed of the wicked shall be cut off.

The righteous shall inherit the land, and dwell therein forever.

The mouth of the righteous speaketh wisdom, and his tongue talketh of judgment.

The law of his God is in his heart; none of his steps shall slide.

Psalms 37 (KJV)

LOVE YOU EACH AND EVERY DAY

Let not your heart be troubled: ye believe in God, believe also in me.
John 14:1 (KJV)

My Son,

Today, I went to PUSH. Jonathan spoke, and he did it well. Busloads of people came from Robbins, Il. I couldn't help but be reminded of Esther, God rest her soul. The city or state is trying to displace over 100 people from their homes to dig a limestone quarry, I think, for a private company. Jonathan lays out the problem so clearly, and yet his family is never there to hear him. So I get the tapes sometimes and I play them in the car for Leah to hear.

Rev's mom often says, "We would do better only if we knew better."

I hope you are eating better? Be sure you eat something green and something alive every day.

Yesterday I forgot to tell you, I've had to look for tiles to repair my bathroom floor. While the guys were dismantling my living room ceiling, they broke about 12 of my new tiles in the bathroom above the living room. My insurance company has sent me from one problem to another.

I am serving on the 42nd reunion committee with Eric Thomas. I am very worried about the success of this project. Eric doesn't realize how much time a project like this requires. He continues to suggest that the failure of a project is really on the shoulders of the committee, not on the head. He is the chairman who selected his committee, and success and failure is on him, the committee head.

Well, I am going to bed.

Please write to me; let me know how you are doing.

Always,
Your loving Mom

November 17, 2013

YOU ARE ALWAYS WITH ME

For God so loved the world, that he gave his only begotten Son, that
whosoever believeth in him should not perish, but have everlasting life.
John 3:16 (KJV)

My Son,

Today I am spending the day at home. That means I am going to try to gain some control over this house. On Monday, I am going to the Chicago Historical Society to see if my house is the oldest in the community. We will see what happens.

How are you? Only when I see you will I know you are being treated well. I have told people we don't hear from you. Why? Many shows about life behind bars are on TV. Often it is very inhumane. I am worried. I am remembering my experience in Puerto Rico. Incarceration wasn't a pleasant experience.

Won't they allow you to communicate? What is going on? I want to see you for myself.

Lovingly,
Mom

I WILL LOVE YOU ALWAYS

My Son,

Count It All Joy!

It is late for me to write tonight. Usually, I draft my letter about 7:00; it is about 11:30. I am normally in bed at this time. But my word is my bond; each day you will hear from me, if only a brief note.

The news was of tornadoes yesterday. Maybe God is still angry about Zimmerman. God's wrath takes its time to take its toll. God is on the throne. What goes around comes around. The God Factor is very real! Keep living.

Rev Evans called tonight. He wants to see you. Put him on your list so he can visit you. I promise I will not seek to send a message to you. You must become God's messenger; I will not try to influence God. You are on your own.

I have been told you said this is like boarding school. One of your "so-called friends" said your wife is very happy, and life is better for your family.

Santita stopped by tonight; we went by Yusef's. Yusef took a flight to Chicago from Atlanta and met Greg Lias's son, who is working at the airport. They were happy to meet. Greg Lias's son is now texting Yusef.

May God bless and keep you,
Mom

NOVEMBER 19, 2013

MY HEART IS WHERE YOU ARE

Put on the whole armour of God,
that ye may be able to stand against the wiles of the devil.
Ephesians 6:11 (KJV)

My Son,

Alanna called me today, first thing this morning. She said she spoke to you, you sounded upbeat, and thanked me for sending you to military school. I am going to pay more attention to things I hear from Washington because I heard that before.

From people in Washington, I hear you are considering doing the full time instead of going in the RDAP Program—which would reduce your sentence. Maybe Marty, Sandi, and Ray are trying to exacerbate your depression. I couldn't stop laughing; then I became sad.

Did you read Tip O'Neill's memoir? I read it some years ago, and I have read some others, but his is the most memorable. He didn't make me question him; he brought laughter and wisdom. Not a lot of confusion. How do you wish for me to proceed with your work?*

Tip O'Neill's memoir is titled *Man of the House*, in case you are interested. I picked up Santita and Bishop Pierson and went to the bookstore.

I love the bookstore. . . . I love the bookstore.

---

* This was a graphic novel that Congressman Jackson was working on in prison.

I brought some books on dehydrating foods. I plan to have a garden, and winter is the time to plan. I love okra and tomatoes, so I will plant more of those vegetables than the others.

I may make some wine & beer. Take care of yourself.

Love,
Mom

I LOVE YOU

Therefore if any man be in Christ, he is a new creature: old things are passed away; behold, all things are become new. And all things are of God, who hath reconciled us to himself by Jesus Christ, and hath given to us the ministry of reconciliation.
II Corinthians 5:17–18 (KJV)

Dear Son,

How are you? Tell me what you do each day. You know the idle mind is the devil's workshop, so catch up on your reading. Perhaps there is a wood shop class that may be of interest. Jesus was a carpenter, and this would be a great hobby since you and I like tools.

Now—for the news or gossip. Ray told my mom he is trying to return to Chicago to work for Quinn & Paul Valas. He said he is willing to work for free; he also told her you are doing very well. Apparently, he is talking to Marty (the so-called Jesse Jr. expert); and Marty is talking to your wife because of the quality of information he has regarding your business.

I have been told by some of our media people that Marty and your wife continue to talk with certain members of the media. Their conversations are not helpful to you.

Maya Angelou said, "When people show you who they are, believe them."

I was told a direct quote, "The household is more tranquil now." The judge "had it in for her," and "she is working on being pardoned." Lots more, I won't write it ever in my letters.

Jonathan said if you can't trust your own friends, then why would he want them? Of course, I feel the same way.

Eddie Ford sent me a plumber today. I have a new garage, and I didn't go to the Chicago History Museum today . . . had to run some other errands.

Don't forget Rev Evans. Richard Thomas died. And Jesse Robinson died also.

I love you very much,
Mom

THINKING OF YOU

If it be possible, as much as lieth in you,
live peaceably with all men.
Romans 12:18 (KJV)

My Son,

I hope all is well for you? Most importantly, I hope you are productive and using your time wisely.

Yusef went with Rev to Washington to attend the award ceremony sponsored by the White House. I think it's the Medal of Freedom Award or something.

Yusef stayed at the house with Mom. She was delighted. Ray stopped by to give Yusef some business advice since he has been in the beer business also.

Mom told me to let you know Ray is selling his parking lots to the condo. He was on the phone in his car, so she overheard the conversation. I think you should move your car. You can use my garage if you wish.

Courtney still comes by to talk with Mom; that helps me a lot.

They finished my garage today, all but placing the door onto it.

The chitterling lady called Santita; she is Fedexing them to her with the recipe so she can cook them. Oh Boy. They will be just as bad as the peach cobbler she makes for Rev. I think I'll go over and pick the chitterlings up and cook them myself.

How much should I pay the lady? She is really, really nice.

We will be eating at Santita's house. Her Christmas trees are already lit.

Going to bed. I hope you are reading the scriptures I send to you. I read them before I write each letter.

Love you very much,
Mom

LOVING YOU ALWAYS

Cast thy burden upon the Lord, and he shall sustain thee:
he shall never suffer the righteous to be moved.
Psalm 55:22 (KJV)

My Son,

The weeks go by so quickly. My mother told me the older you grow, the faster time passes. I have lived long enough to realize the saying is true. Soon it will be Christmas, tax time, and then Christmas again.

I fell down my stairs and broke my toe again. I have broken my toes so many times, I now know how to bandage the toes together and save myself $385.00—it may be more today. But that was what it used to cost.

By the way, based on my personal survey, on the average, 4 to 6 people come to me each day, when I am in public, to wish you well or inquire about your well-being. God is good. These acts of kindness renew my faith. I thank God for his blessings.

I am always happy to write you each day. I am getting used to it now. I hope receiving my letters brings you joy, and connects you to a familiar space filled with love, hope, and peace.

Yvonne Travis, who says she is bipolar, called today. She's coming for Thanksgiving. We will be happy to see her.

Allene sends Mrs. Malone a check each month. We have been doing this for about 11 years. The check came back yesterday, and her number is no longer working. This doesn't look good.

I had to call the boys, Noah & Jonathan, to help me bring the groceries into the house tonight. I am glad we are neighbors.
Nothing else.

Love you,
Mom

November 23, 2013

THINKING OF YOU

Casting all your care upon him; for he careth for you.
I Peter 5:7 (KJV)

Dear Son,

I hope your spirit is high and you are reading the scriptures I share with you. Things are okay, but it is very cold.

I shopped for groceries today; at least 9 strangers asked about you. At least, I believe, 7 were sincere; the others just wanted to have something to talk about. They also expressed, repeatedly, their unhappiness with your situation. Jo Bee called to cheer me up, but started to cry for 15 minutes. She said she just doesn't know what to do; she wants to see you. We both have friends nearby; she wants me to come down, stay with them, and then come see you. That's a lot of time.

Many are angry. Especially when the Congressman in Florida was caught, and I was told by media, taped purchasing over $200.00 worth of cocaine—and was given probation and allowed to keep his seat, while others are serving time for doing the same thing.

Several people have called to tell us of a Congressman who sent his daughter to college with his campaign fund and is still sitting comfortably in Congress.

Others are allowed to pay back millions of dollars to the government after causing the loss of people's pension, homes, jobs, and for many, their quality of life. Yet when Yusef asked that we—or you—be allowed to pay back the fund to your campaign, which you raised, we were told NO!

It is sad to know many of us are witnessing the disparities between rich and poor, upper class and underclass, those on the inside and those on the outside.

The very worst that has happened in our alleged civil society is hunger and homelessness.

To close schools, knowing children go there to get a hot breakfast and lunch with no other food options is by far the most inhuman act I have heard. Curses, curses, curses on all who have participated in this heartless act.

I thank God for the many information networks . . . the truth is becoming clearer & closer.

It's called the God Factor. When there is a gap, God will step in.

The scripture says God is not the author of confusion. And the thief comes to steal, kill, and destroy; but God comes so that we may have life and have it more abundantly.[1] And if life has not the abundance of food, clothing, shelter, truthfulness, love, and peace, it is not of God.

Now some clarity for you . . . I love you today more than I did the day you were born. When I think of you, I smile and my heart is warmed. God protects you and loves you.

You broke man's rule, which man calls the law.

When I lived in Fort Pierce, Florida as a child, the police would come to the houses of blacks and they would shout, "Open the door in the name of the law!" as they kicked in the door—without a search warrant. They were all white. "The Law" was segregation, discrimination, and any act of intimidation that helped to maintain low achievement and low aspirations. These rules helped create "laws that maintained the status quo," not justice, not fairness, and certainly not peace—but business as usual.

I saw this, you didn't. I am not deceived. I don't want you to be confused about rules & laws. God has Law, man has rules . . . Only a perfect spirit can create Laws.

As a child I was taught, "In all that you do, remember the Golden Rule: 'Do unto others as you would have them do unto you.'"[2] This is God's Law that man has made into a rule.

Have you ever seen the implementation of this Rule/Law domestically, internationally, politically, spiritually, etc.? No, you haven't!

We don't teach that Law anymore. It is too perfect and Godly.

If God's Law prevailed, a man could not shoot a child—an unarmed child—in cold blood and leave the courtroom exonerated, with his pistol at his side. The man in Detroit shoots a girl child in the face, while she's on his porch seeking help, and only the public's outcry is cause for a potential investigation. In Florida, a football player seeking help because his car broke down, is shot down by police. I can go on and on. We are functioning by man's rules and everything is upside down. Man is imperfect; he can't make Laws, only imperfect rules.

Jesse, God will prevail. I want you to examine God's Laws and stay with them. My mother would say, when she would whip me and I would scream, "You're gonna be glad I am whipping your— instead of God." I didn't understand until I received a couple of beatings from God.

Now, to tell you the truth, of my mother's whippings I remember my screams; of God's beatings I know "the why," and I still feel the pain.

Hold on to God. God is real . . . you will see.

Mom

NOVEMBER 24, 2013

I LOVE YOU

Passing through the street near her corner;
and he went the way to her house.
Proverbs 7:8 (KJV)

Son,

Jackie passed her exam. She is now a candidate for her PhD. She is very happy, and so am I. God is Good.

I love you from head to toe.

On my way to Richard Thomas's funeral, I had to wear sandals in this cold weather because of my broken toes, and I'm sure everyone is going to think I am crazy.

I was turning the TV off, and I saw Pastor Andrew D. Singleton Jr. of Victory Apostolic Church, 20801 Matteson Ave, Matteson, IL 60443. So I am writing him a letter tonight; can't spend much time on your letter.

His message was on "Having an Attitude of Gratitude," Luke 17:18–19. He spoke about ungrateful people. So I am writing him tonight, and I am sending something for the church.

You should write him; he will be glad to hear from you. Please thank his church for their support.

Got to go to see Richard off.

I love you,
Mom

THINKING OF YOU

And if we know that he hear us, whatsoever we ask,
we know that we have the petitions that we desired of him.
I John 5:15 (KJV)

Dear Son,

My day began very early. I had to be at grandparent's day at 7:30 for Yusef Jr. Of course, I was late, and I forgot my glasses. When you forget your glasses and can't see, people think you are illiterate. So always keep your glasses with you. Once you've explained you don't have your glasses with you and ask someone to read the name on the bottle or the instructions on the wall, they read it to you slowly, then pause and ask if you understand what they read. Maybe because I am old and can't see, young people think I am crazy. They ask are you out by yourself? Are you alone? Should I call someone for you?

I started to stop by the pancake house at breakfast, but received a call to return home. The people working on my house were outside and needed access to the inside of the house. They bang all day long.

I think I told you I sent a contribution to Pastor Singleton's church. I like his and Rev Winston's ministries.

LOVING YOU ALWAYS

"Let No One Have Power Over You But God."
—Mrs. Passmore

My God, This has been a great day.

The men are working in the house. I am cooking. I am with you all the time, and everyone I care about is well.

Thanks Be to God!

This Is My Best Letter,
Mom

LOVE

For God so loved the world, that he gave his only begotten Son, that whosoever believeth in him should not perish, but have everlasting life.
John 3:16 (KJV)

My Son,

All is well. I went to Costco this morning, first thing. I enjoy going to the Clyborne store because the staff is high-spirited. They make shopping with them a pleasure. There is a lady there whose name is Percola; she is from Mississippi. She always asks about you.

I stopped by PUSH and then went to Yusef's to make a banana pudding.

Yvonne Travis is in town; she left a pound cake at my door.

Jackie is coming over; she stopped by Bettye Odom's first.

I've got to do my cooking now.

I love you very much,
Mom

LOVING YOU ALWAYS

For all have sinned, and come short of the glory of God.
Romans 3:23 (KJV)

Dear Son,

I love you very much. Jackie came home. She looks great. We spent time talking about school. She has her schedule for graduation now, and she is excited. So am I.

She is sounding more and more like a Michigan Republican—but a progressive Black Republican. This is bringing diversity to our political conversations.

Today I am finishing my cooking; must be at Santita's by 2:30.

Rev is pensive about his arrangements to see you because of the threat of a storm.

You know Santita never wants to host dinners. She told someone I pushed this on her. She doesn't like company either.

I will get through this with a lot of prayer.

I will return late tonight because Sandy is going out of town Saturday; and we will have to clean her place from top to bottom or never hear the last of this experience for the rest of our natural lives.

Will write more tomorrow.

Love you very, very much,
Mom

THINKING OF YOU

Jesus Wept.
John 11:35 (KJV)

My Son,

Thanksgiving was almost uneventful until your call. My, you have no idea how happy we were to hear your voice. I have no words to express the excitement in our hearts. Thank you for calling—it means so much.

Bettye O and her next-door neighbor stopped by. Rae Lewis, who is always our centerpiece, spent the holiday with us.

Yusef, Amaya, and all the grands were present, but you were not there, and we missed your presence, so we didn't laugh as much. Jonathan brought one of his students from Ecuador to dine with us. He knows the school that Susan managed. He was pleasant.

My mother called me and asked for your phone number. She wants to call you sometimes. She doesn't understand any of this.

Everything was small talk this Thanksgiving, which is most unusual for us.

Jonathan fried catfish for us. It was the very best I have ever had. He soaked it in buttermilk, and it was wonderful. Rae brought her dog. The children chased and worried me and the dog the entire evening.

After you called, Rae and all of us spent the best of the evening laughing about you and the good times, like when you tried to give Rhoda her room and Ray Anderson—who wanted Rae to hem his pants, etc.

It was big fun.

I will come to see you when I return to Washington. That will be soon. I love you.

Lots of love for you,
Mom

P.S. I've been in bed most of the day.

December 1, 2013

LOVING YOU

For the wages of sin is death; but the gift of God
is eternal life through Jesus Christ our Lord.
Romans 6:23 (KJV)

My Son,

I am in constant prayer for you. I am sorry I placed your letters in my purse and forgot to mail them. I remembered when I got home. You know how cheap I am. Picking my vegetables and freezing them; junk stores; sales that I love . . . I can't bring myself to spend money on stamps. That's why I try to send three letters for one stamp.

Hope you enjoyed your father and brother's visit. They were so excited to see you. Rev didn't talk too much about his visit, and I haven't spoken with Jonathan yet. I texted him yesterday so he can come over—you know Jonathan, I'll hear from him whenever.

Spent the day with Leah. We have decided to diet together. She's taking photography lessons on Saturdays. I pick her up, and we go to lunch or shopping.

I spoke with Amaya. I am going to help her with Yusef. He is poking his tongue out and kicking at people. I told her we will have to pull him in. He must be taught respect, and he will love us for it.

The meanest parent is the best parent.

She told me she wants me to help.

Please reach out to Jonathan; he really needs you. There is a sadness inside of him. Something is wrong. Will you help him? I don't care if you tell him I am concerned. Thank you.

I love you much,
Mom

DECEMBER 2, 2013

LOVING YOU

For all have sinned, and come short of the glory of God.
Romans 3:23 (KJV)

My Son,

I hope the scriptures I select for you are not a waste of my time. I want you to look up the scriptures and examine their meaning and allow God's Word to impact your life, so you may help others. Most of all, I am hoping you let God's Word have power over you and everyone you are with.

God can. It's left up to you.

Today was a slow day. I have been tired as of late. It may be my foot or the change in the weather.

Rev is in Europe; he will return on Friday.

Please don't forget to pray,
Mom

LOVING YOU

My Son,

Hearing your voice this morning was, for me, the sound of music. Still can't find the words to express my joy.

When I found your letter in the mailbox last night, I thought that was as good as it could get. But this morning, the Lord blessed me with your voice, and that was the best yet!

I am happy, happy, happy. I won't read your letter until I find a quiet moment, probably when I catch the train to Washington Wednesday. Mom has to go home to turn her heat on and spend a few days with her friends. Chris is going to drive down with us, I think. Before your wife and kids visited you, Ray told Gertie they were coming. How did he know?

Ray's girlfriend is very pregnant. She is a very nice person. I hope this works this time and that she will help him become his best self. She has found a job; he hasn't, and they're not married yet. Both of them are not children: he is 50 something? I will tell you more tomorrow. I love you.

Mom

THINKING OF YOU

For Christ is the end of the law for righteousness to every one that believeth.
Romans 10:4 (KJV)

My Son,

My son, as you see, I am writing you free handed and without editing. Many of my thoughts may not appear completed, and often some words are misspelled. But I am trying to keep my promise: a letter a day.

So forgive me. Most of my letters are the first drafts without editing.

When you return, please allow me to correct my letters because I believe you will probably keep them, and I want them to be well-written for my grandchildren.

Please read this scripture. God always keeps his promise.

I am on the train to Washington, thinking of you with love in my heart for you.

How are you? Yvonne Travis was in town . . . spent time with her. She sends her love, and she brought a cake over to the house. Her daddy is 80 something and still working, and her mother is doing fine. I forgot to give Bettye Odom your address; she has asked me for it twice. When I return, I must remember to take it to her house.

I was told your wife and children came to see you. I know you were happy to see them. Remember, we talked about the inclusion of your children on the matter.

I am certain this is not a healthy approach to their emotional development. If your condition becomes an acceptable state of existence, it will be a bad example for them. Now, if you are a bad example, you are discredited. To your children, you can't be viewed as a bad example or weak. This doesn't give either parent an advantage.

It is now time for both of you to grow up. Stop the games. The children are at risk or at stake here. You know, you are not being spoken of well at your home. You Know That! You think there is pain in male/female relationships. Well, let me tell you, you haven't had pain until you witness the pain a child brings to their parents. That is a pain no one wishes on people they don't even like.

Now, here is the deal.

Jesse, I learned from my mother how to do this. Had my mother left my stepdad, I am sure I never would have been able to stay married. To this day, my mom doesn't know she showed me how to do this—we learn by example. She also told me my friends should be married women, and you have witnessed my friends. My true friends have been married or widowed women. The role of the mother is key.

You said you wished I had pursued an active career. I did. My choice was to be a good mother—first; wife—second; supporter—third; person—fourth. In that order.

I guess I should say mother-wife, or wife-mother.

In my marriage, I had to make a choice. I love your dad and always will. I have proven it to him by supporting him and being loyal to him.

Down through the years, it has not been easy.

When he became a handful, I have maintained my loyalty to him and undaunted support of him and his work.

Now, he can't stop thanking me. I tell him I have only done my duty.

Now, if a young mother has had no example of a constant man in her mother's life, she will forever have a problem—a problem no man will be able to solve. Period. And any man trying to close that gap will soon be destroyed also.

Children don't deserve to be victimized by parents' foolish behavior. Then what do you do?

Pray for strength and courage to do what you must do to save your children.

I am giving advice I have used.

I stopped trying to save my marriage and decided to save my family.

I had to move over with your dad and let God go get him, and I am glad I did. Relationships with men must be normalized, or I am afraid children, too, will drift into this cycle of confusion.

Jessica and her relationship with men must be normalized; or I am afraid she, too, will drift into this cycle of confusion, as will your son.

Your child can hurt you far worse than your wife could ever hurt you. Personally, old women told me this; and I listened.

So my goal became to do all I could for my husband. But my primary goal was to save my children.

That's why I was long on patience with him and very low on tolerance for poor behavior from my children.

You and your wife don't have to make it, but your children must!

At some point, I don't know when, I turned my husband and marriage over to God and accepted its fate. I concentrated all my prayers and effort on saving my children.

That's why I placed you in schools. And I drove alone for miles to LeMans, down those long dark country roads, to participate with you on birthdays, ball games, etc. St. Albans, or whatever school you all attended, was my trying to save each one of you. I did it by myself. I have, Jesse, no regrets. I did my best.

Children do what their parents do, so be very careful. Don't confuse them.

This letter, written on the train, consists of 16 pages and notes. To be continued . . .

I will always love you,
Mom

P.S. I may repeat myself in my next letter if I get lost in my notes.

DECEMBER 5, 2013

THINKING OF YOU

Not that I speak in respect of want: for I have learned,
in whatsoever state I am, therewith to be content.
Philippians 4:11 (KJV)

My Son,

I have arrived in Washington. I am now more tired than I was when I got on the train. This trip was a ride through hell.

An old white man, an ex–Navy Seal, got mad because he couldn't figure out which door to exit so he could get off to smoke. So he took a seat next to a white woman to complain . . . became very familiar, felt her breast, and all hell broke loose.

He was subdued at the lower car by the conductors and a male passenger, who discovered the ex–Navy Seal had a pistol in his pocket as they held him on the floor of the car.

The train stopped; the police were there outside of Toledo to receive him. He went into their car without handcuffs. Now, I can tell you, I have seen with my own eyes, black men less violent on the train who were roughed up, handcuffed, and arrested—and they were not armed with a firearm. There is a difference.

Then, the young grandma behind me with her grandson by her 21-year-old daughter (who got pregnant and decided to have the baby while unmarried), talked on the phone to her boyfriend all the way to Washington, DC.

She asked me to babysit twice because she needed a break. I obliged . . . my, my, my. If this wasn't enough to drive me crazy,

[60]

an obnoxious man sat across from me and wanted to know if I was spoken for.

I am home . . . tired. Just heard about Mandela and saw you with him on TV while in South Africa for his release.

Bettye Magness's grandson . . . shot seven times on the way to the store. He didn't make it.

I love you,
Mom

DECEMBER 6, 2013

LOVING YOU

There hath no temptation taken you but such as is common to man:
but God is faithful, who will not suffer you to be tempted above
that ye are able; but will with the temptation also make a way
to escape, that ye may be able to bear it.
I Corinthians 10:13 (KJV)

My Son,

Stayed home most of the day with echoes of Mandela everywhere. I am so glad we were there when he was released. Did I tell you I saw you on the balcony with him? I spent the rest of the night laughing at you climbing the rails and fences up to the choice spot. I love you. Ray posted your picture on his page.

Had dinner with Kevin Gray; he wants to come to see you. He is working with prisoners. His number is xxx-xxx-xxxx. I think he is teaching in one of the prisons or out-programs in South Carolina. I went to dinner with Ray, Kevin, and Mr. Corry.

I love you.

You must not forget: it was the efforts of Winnie that freed Mandela.

DECEMBER 7, 2013

LOVING YOU

Wherefore, holy brethren, partakers of the heavenly calling, consider
the Apostle and High Priest of our profession, Christ Jesus.
Hebrews 3:1 (KJV)

My Son,

Fix Your Thoughts on Jesus.

I have just returned from taking Gertie to Virginia to turn her heat on and to let her water drip slowly, so her pipes won't burst.

She fussed all the way because we left late. Dara went with me; she calms her down a bit.

Jonny Savory called. He attended Rev Barrow's birthday party tonight, so I sang "Happy Birthday" to her. You should send her a note to PUSH; she always asks about you.

Everyone asks about you.

Please send my mom a note. She would love that you know she is 86 and loves you.

I have not heard or read any news today.

Many are preparing to go to South Africa.

I won't be going because of my broken toe. I don't want anything to happen to it.

I love you too much.

It's about 11:00 p.m., goodnight. Tim Schools wants your number. I'll send it to him.

All my love,
Mom

DECEMBER 8, 2013

LOVING YOU

That if thou shalt confess with thy mouth the Lord, Jesus, and shalt believe in thine heart that God hath raised him from the dead, thou shalt be saved.
Romans 10:9 (KJV)

My Son,

How are you?

I woke up late today. There is snow on the trees; what a beautiful sight. I love the snow and the winter.

I am not going to South Africa. I can't risk reinjuring my toe.

I am sick to my stomach hearing the many lies people are telling about their relationship with Mandela.

I did not know Mandela was taken off America's terrorist list in 2008 on July 1—by Bush, not Clinton. All the while, Winnie Mandela was left on the terrorist list.

The media continue to say Mandela was in jail for 27 years, not that he was in jail for life.

America, and our role in hurting the people of South Africa, is an embarrassment before the world. When will we learn?

Will write more the next time.

Love always,
Mom

THINKING OF YOU

*But if we walk in the light, as he is in the light, we
have fellowship one with another, and the blood of
Jesus Christ his Son cleanseth us from all sin.*
I John 1:7 (KJV)

My Son,

I think of you every day.

I won't write much today . . . spent most of the day watching
Mandela on TV. *Frontline* had a wonderful personal story. It cleared
the air for me with my ill feelings as to why Mandela quit Winnie.
Now I have heard why he left, I am still sad. If you get a chance,
try to watch the *Frontline* piece. I think it is called, "The Long Walk
Home." It is a very informative piece or story. They also told how
they taped all of his conversations . . . Even the trees were bugged.

I am going to bed now. Will write more next time.

Love you,
Mom

December 10, 2013

THINKING OF YOU

*All we like sheep have gone astray; we have turned every one to his
own way; and the Lord hath laid on him the iniquity of us all.*
Isaiah 53:6 (KJV)

My Son,

How are you?

All the world today is Mandela! I am happy he has made it into
that place in history for those who have made the greatest sacrifice
of selflessness. To lay down one's life for his fellow man . . . is the
greatest deed.

You realize how long I have been angry with Mandela for leaving Winnie; but after the *Frontline* piece, I am even more sad.

I saw Winnie today—her demeanor was unrecognizable. The
Winnie I have known through the years has always been poised,
with zeal, passion, and self-assurance. She always radiated a level
of confidence that was contagious and electrifying. This morning
when I saw her, my heart hurt for her. She appeared defeated and
confused.

I felt her loss to be greater than just Mandela's death, but that and
the death of their togetherness.

The *Frontline* story spent time discussing their relationship,
which helped me understand his dilemma.

The documentary said the relationship was strained because of
her infidelity. It seems while he was in prison, there were rumors;
and Mandela had defended her honor as best he could.

I had excused her behavior because he was jailed for life. A life sentence should allow some exceptions.

Then, here is another dilemma. If Winnie believed the movement would be victorious, then would her conduct reflect a wife anxious for her husband's return or release?

That, in itself, created conflicting messages to the people. For a while, she stopped visiting Mandela at the prison. When he was released, she continued her behavior. The final straw was a visit to the USA: A tour that he pleaded with her not to take. The report said, "He begged her not to take."

He, Mandela, called the hotel late at night and the man she was accused of seeing answered the phone. Then all hell broke loose. Mandela left her after she pleaded with him not to.

Now my opinion was shaped by the interview I saw one night. Winnie said, "My husband has forgiven all those who have hurt our people, yet he has no space in his heart to forgive me."

Her words shaped for me a very negative opinion of Mr. Mandela. However, upon learning this new information, I don't see how he would have maintained the respect of his peers with such an uncontrollable situation.

I now understand what he did. Otherwise, his effectiveness would have been diminished.

Now, I regret having judged him. Winnie's strength, and her independence, began to weaken his and her purpose.

A purposeful life is always larger than the person. A personal life is always the size of the person.

The God Factor . . .

Mr. Mandela was in prison for 27 years without contact with the outside world. Mrs. Winnie Mandela was his voice.

History must say it was her guidance and leadership that lead to the freedom of Mandela and his country.

Only God can take a crooked stick and hit a straight lick.

My Love, My Heart . . .

My thoughts are always with you,
Mom

December 11, 2013

LOVING YOU

Blessed be the God and Father of our Lord Jesus Christ, which
according to his abundant mercy hath begotten us again unto a lively
hope by the resurrection of Jesus Christ from the dead.
I Peter 1:3 (KJV)

My Son,

I hope you are doing fine. I hope you are reading and writing.

Last night, I went to dinner with Ray and Mr. Corry. It's a new Thai place on 14th St. Henry Gates was there, we spoke. He expressed his concern for you and said he would like to visit you. I think he was sincere. He was very engaging.

Today I got my toes done, redeemed some coupons, watched the news, and did some knitting. Oh, also, the card I sent . . . I don't remember when I received it. But I am sure it was from someone who cares.

Will write more tomorrow.

Love you,
Mom

THINKING OF YOU

The Lord is my Shepherd.
Psalm 23:1 (KJV)

My Son,

How are you?

Short note today. Last night, about 2:00 a.m., I saw a special on Butner Correctional Facilities.

The subject was Mr. Madoff's place of residence, so we were given a tour of the facilities. It is a very large institution. Is it a correctional or punishment institution? Is there a school? I did see that there is a library. I think they said there is a law library. Do you go there often?

I love you, and I am very proud of you. So many people say wonderful things about you; and when you leave this place, I expect the people in there to know what a good person you are.

Now always remember the Golden Rule: "Do unto others as you would have them do unto you."[1]

Remember the M&M's: Your Morals & Manners.

Love you so much,
Mom

P.S. I want to see you before Christmas with my mom. Let me know.

December 12, 2013

A Psalm of David

The Lord is my shepherd;
I have all that I need.
He lets me rest in green meadows;
he leads me beside peaceful streams.
He renews my strength.
He guides me along right paths,
bringing honor to his name.
Even when I walk
through the darkest valley,
I will not be afraid,
for you are close beside me.
Your rod and your staff
protect and comfort me.
You prepare a feast for me
in the presence of my enemies.
You honor me by anointing my head with oil.
My cup overflows with blessings.
Surely your goodness and unfailing love will pursue me
all the days of my life,
and I will live in the house of the Lord forever.

Psalms 23 (KJV)

December 13, 2013

THINKING OF YOU

Ye shall diligently keep the commandments of the Lord your God, and his testimonies, and his statutes, which he hath commanded thee.
Deuteronomy 6:17 (KJV)

My Son,

I hope every night you pray. If you are not praying as I do, I will be very disappointed.

God is good and does answer prayers. We must be careful of the prayers we pray. When you wanted to go to Congress, I asked God to grant you your wish. To show my gratitude, I promised God that on the day your wish was granted I would stop smoking. During that period, I was smoking two packs of Winstons a day, sometimes without the filter.

When your votes came in that November 3, I smoked my last cigarette. I stopped smoking that night. I have never made a promise to God that I didn't keep; and God has never made a promise to me that wasn't kept.

I thank God for loving you and making you a loving person. Your heart is good, and God is going to guide you if you let God do it.

Jesse, we make many stops and turns on life's journey.

Your faith can grow stronger. Where you are, you have the space and time to grow in God's grace.

Take your time, we are all waiting for you. Patience is the only virtue that you need to strengthen.

Patience is practiced every day.

Now, how to begin?

1. Allow me to think about this or that.
2. I'll get back to you.
3. Let me first calm down (I say this the most to myself).

Sometimes I use my favorite lines inspired by *Gone with the Wind*: "I am not going to worry my pretty little head," and "I'll think about it tomorrow, because tomorrow is another day."

My other favorite line is, "Frankly, my dear, I don't give a damn."[1] Of course, this line must be whispered under your breath.

These are great lines that give you time to put things in perspective.

Your father has always had patience, tons of it. I am sure you have never paid that much attention to this quality he has because he was gone so much, or you were away at school. I have much love and respect for him. Perhaps because he exercises so much patience, it frightens me. I have so much respect for his goodness and his unquestionable love for people. You know beyond a shadow of a doubt I love your father, and I love you and my entire family.

May God bless all of you at Butner.

Love,
Mom

P.S. I pray for the people there also.

December 14, 2013

LOVING YOU ALWAYS

Remember the former things of old: for I am God, and there is none else;
I am God, and there is none like me, Declaring the end from the
beginning, and from ancient times the things that are not yet done,
saying, My counsel shall stand, and I will do all my pleasure.
Isaiah 46: 9-10 (KJV)

My Son,

Love you.

It's a little chilly. You know I like the cold.

I painted the stairs today, and I had to stop to go pick up some paint thinner.

I passed Bible Way Church. The church is celebrating their 86th anniversary. The large sign on the building said the sermon is, "Back to the Future"; Isaiah 46:9-10. I haven't read it yet, but I am including it in this letter because it will bring good cheer.

I will read this scripture before I go to bed.

It's raining. Mom and I went to Costco; she fussed all the way there and back. She's having a terrible time with her right foot.

Make sure you eat lots of vegetables. Remember the body is alive . . . you must eat something fresh each day.

THINKING OF YOU

For mine eyes have seen thy salvation,
Which thou hast prepared before the face of all people.
Luke 2:30-31 (KJV)

My Son,

I watched the funeral of Mandela today and nodded off occasionally.

I texted Jessica about your Christmas request. She said she wants something from Urban Outfitters or iTunes gift certificates, and Jesse wants a new video game.

Ray stopped by to see Mom. All is well, will write more when I know more.

What shall I do about the children? Waiting to hear from you.

Keeping my mind on Christ.

Love you much,
Mom

LOVING YOU

Let us therefore come boldly unto the throne of grace, that we may
obtain mercy, and find grace to help in time of need.
Hebrews 4:16 (KJV)

My Son,

Don't forget to pray.

Mr. Corry, Dara, and I spent most of the day visiting a new store called Wegmans. It was a great shopping experience. Mr. Corry took me to pick up some fresh greens. I'll cook them tomorrow.

Please write your friend who sent the chitterlings and tell her how much we enjoyed them. They were as good as you said.

My sister came into Washington unexpectedly late. We sat and talked the greater part of the evening from 11:00 p.m. until about 2:30 a.m. So I am writing you very late tonight. I am very happy my sister is here.

She reminded me Cynthia has been gone 10 years. My brother has been gone 8 yrs.

Their lives—so short-lived. Time goes by so quickly, and I truly miss them. Sometimes Cynthia still makes me laugh aloud.

I texted Jessica today; she said she wants a certificate from Urban Outfitters. I need to know what video Tre wants.

I mean Jesse. We must call him by his name.

All is well.

May God keep you,
Mom

THINKING OF YOU

And if I go and prepare a place for you, I will come again, and receive
you unto myself; that where I am, there ye may be also.
John 14:3 (KJV)

My Son,

Today I cooked my greens. Connie and I shared them. Sometimes you just get a taste for greens, isn't that odd? I hope you are eating vegetables.

I got the gift for Jessica. I think I should just give Jesse a Best Buy certificate. What do you think?

Rev has not returned to the States yet. Yusef arrived this morning. He felt good about the experience. I don't know if Jonathan was with them . . . will find that out when I return to Chicago.

I may not see you before Christmas. I still have pressing problems in Chicago that I must attend to. Please send a message about what to do about the children.

I love you.
Mom

December 18, 2013

And there was one Anna, a prophetess, the daughter of Phanuel, of the tribe of Aser: she was of a great age, and had lived with an husband seven years from her virginity; And she was a widow of about fourscore and four years, which departed not from the temple, but served God with fastings and prayers night and day. And she coming in that instant gave thanks likewise unto the Lord, and spake of him to all them that looked for redemption in Jerusalem.
Luke 2:36–38 (KJV)

My Son,

My mother says this house runs on shifts; one group comes in and another group leaves. Today was just that kind of day.

As you can see, my scripture has nothing to do with my letter.

Rev is still in Africa. Yusef read to me the children's Christmas request.

I was proud to know Jessica loves to read. That's very nice to know. Now you must think twice about Jesse's video game request. The earphones are so popular, the phones may place them in harm's way. I would not get them for Noah several years ago. He has never forgiven me.

People are taking these headphones from people, and children are not aware of others while wearing them out.

Writing is very difficult in the house with mom and Connie fussing all day.

J. C. Hayward has been taken off the television; seems as though she is in some trouble with a charter school. I know J. C. Hayward, and I have reached out to her. There is no way I am going to believe she waited to become this experienced to do something crazy. She has said she wants her name cleared.

But I know something is very wrong when the many blacks who care for other blacks and have been accountable to them are all now in trouble. I smell a rat. The timing of all of this is not good.

Love you sincerely,
Mom

December 19, 2013

LOVING YOU VERY MUCH

To open their eyes, and to turn them from darkness to light, and from the power of Satan unto God, that they may receive forgiveness of sins, and inheritance among them which are sanctified by faith that is in me.
Acts 26:18 (KJV)

My Son,

How are you? We were trying to see you for Christmas, but it didn't work this time. I am returning to Chicago next week.

I will try again when I return back East.

Did you receive the pictures from Mr. Corry?

It feels like summer outside. Connie decided to rake my leaves, while I looked on.

Ray stops by often. He is helpful with my mother. He stops by and checks on Mom and introduces her to other young people. For that I am grateful.

You know she talks everybody to death. Today she is pouting because of the fight she had with Connie. Now you know my sister?

By the way, I have decided to get Jesse a gift certificate to Best Buy. I will pick it up tomorrow.

Will write you tomorrow.

May God bless and keep you,
Mom

December 20, 2013

THINKING OF YOU

He will keep the feet of his saints, and the wicked shall be silent
in darkness for by strength shall no man prevail.
I Samuel 2:9 (KJV)

My Son,

This scripture I had to write, so you don't have to look it up.

Ray has sold the parking spaces. You should move your car. I don't care what they say.

CK called this morning and told me you will not be alone on Christmas. I am happy to know that, very happy.

I will put the kids' gifts in the mail tomorrow because the only seat available before Christmas on the train to Chicago leaves Saturday.

I've heard there is a storm coming. Perhaps sometime in January I will see you.

I also just found out your family is always on the list . . . is that true? Try to eat vegetables.

Don't forget to pray. Please pray with your children and for them.

God bless you and all those who care for you.

Love you,
Mom

DECEMBER 21, 2013

˙ LOVING YOU

My Son,

How are you? Don't forget the Golden Rule.

While clearing some old papers, I came across these priceless prayers I used in speeches in '84. I hope you find them useful.

Lord make me an instrument of your peace,

Where there is hatred, let me sow love.

Where there is doubt, faith.

Where there is despair, hope.

Where there is darkness, light.

And where there is sadness, joy.

Prayer of Saint Francis Assisi (Peace Prayer)[1]

"I have swum against the currents of the time."[2]

I'll Always Love You,
Mom

DECEMBER 23, 2013

THINKING OF YOU

Thy mercy, O Lord, is in the heavens;
and thy faithfulness reacheth unto the clouds.
Psalm 36:5

My Son,

How are you?

While out today, I received an excited Rae Lewis phone call. That is the best I can explain her enthusiasm.

She was so very excited to receive a letter from you. Her joy is so infectious.

Rev returned from Africa today. This may have been his longest stay away from home, ever.

He said he has never been so homesick in his life, but he said he learned a lot. As for South Africa, there will be some difficult days ahead, he said. From South Africa he went on to Nigeria. Nigeria is fascinating for Rev. Since the '60s we have in some way inter-acted and known many of their leaders personally. So he knows the landscape.

He spent lots of time with Winnie and the new Mrs. Mandela. He has some wonderful stories to share.

After the holidays, I will write more.

Love you,
Mom

DECEMBER 24, 2013

LOVING YOU SO MUCH

Behold, I am the Lord, the God of all flesh:
is there any thing too hard for me?
Jeremiah 32:27 (KJV)

My Son,

How are you? Fine, I hope. I have lots of cooking ahead of me. The boys agreed they would cook all the meats, and I am to cook the vegetables, but we will not have a real Christmas without you.

I hope your family is there, as I heard they would be for the holiday. Jackie is staying at the house with me. Santita has just returned from Detroit. She was worried to death about coming down to be with you. She almost drove me crazy and certainly would have driven you nuts also. *Roots* has been on TV all day. It is now 10:00 p.m., and I have just about had enough. I didn't know there were so many episodes.

Merry Christmas with love,
Mom

I'LL BE LOVING YOU ALWAYS

And I was afraid, and went and hid thy talent in the earth:
lo, there thou hast that is thine.
Matthew 6:25 (KJV)

My Son,

It's Christmas day! I am happy that God so loved the world that He gave His only begotten Son and that man has the sense to celebrate His birth. Some of the Happy Holiday advocates made me upset. I said loudly, "If you want just a 'Happy Holiday,' I am going to stop shopping." This woman said, "OH NO! We just say this not to offend others." And yet they offend me! "No way," I said, "I am going to be more vocal about not shopping, and let's see how everyone feels about a holiday without Jesus."

I am going over to Yusef's to help him and Amaya with the beef roast and banana pudding. I think they could manage without me now that we have the Internet, with all the recipes on it. I think they need me for little Yusef, who is the oldest and a handful . . . and so am I when the two of us are together.

One day, Yusef asked me to come over and play with the children. But I told him I don't play with little children because they don't know how to stop playing. Adults never really played with me; however, my mom taught me how to jump double-dutch and how to turn the ropes. At that time, I must have been 6 or 7 years old, and she may have been 20. Children hitting you, while you assume they're trying to play with you, is a way they have for testing your tolerance. When they want to wrestle and tussle with you, they are testing your strength. Playing is very confusing to them; and they often don't understand when the play has ended and is growing out of control. And you become angry and harsh with them when you have created the confusion.

So, when you shout at them, they shout back at you; when you tell them "No," they tell you "No"—and ofttimes throw a tantrum. And when you strike them, attempting to gain control once again, they strike you back. In a situation like this, my mother used to say, "You have put yourself in a position for your child to whip your behind very soon."

Lavell called. He calls every holiday. He has a job now and is very excited about it. He's coming to visit this summer. I have always loved him.

This Christmas is not the same without you. There were no festivities, just the meal and light chitchat. This Christmas I made three types of corn bread: crackling; Spanish; and plain. My bread wasn't a hit. We did have too much food.

Jackie and I have returned from Yusef's. Skye and Leah are off to New York with Marilyn tomorrow.

Bobby Dallas called, wants to write you. I love you so much.

May God bless and keep you,
Mom

THINKING OF YOU

Giving thanks always for all things unto God
and the Father in the name of our Lord Jesus Christ.
Ephesians 5:20 (KJV)

My Son,

How are you? Rev is once again excited about visiting you.

Tonight Rev was able to talk with your wife. He said he has tried many times to find her.

I stopped by your house, before leaving Washington, two times to give the gift cards; no one was at home. I still have the certificates.

Jackie and I spent the greater part of the day talking about her graduation and her future.

She is very excited about her PhD, and so am I.

We were called at about 11:00 to join Rev, Yusef, Skye, and Yusef's four boys at Gibson's for Skye's going-away trip to join Marilyn and her children in NY.

Skye also received a sewing machine for Christmas. So we are going to make a skirt. I am excited.

Amaya is leaving tomorrow for Canada with the children. Yusef will stay here to finish his business and join them for a few days.

All is well.

I love and miss you so much,

Mom

UNDATED #1

My Son,

How are you?

I just received your letters today, and as always, I am overjoyed to hear from you. Please know you are not alone, you are loved. We will help as we have always tried. You must not worry, we will do the things you've requested to keep your family afloat.

Strangely, Christmas, we discussed pulling together some funds for Sandi and the children. I know you don't want to hear this, but this is our situation.

Jonathan has three children in private school, and Yusef doesn't have his money yet. He bundled everything to make the company larger, so he is not at his financial capacity at this time.

The company won't officially be sold until January or February. Now, I am not waiting on his money . . . just explaining the financial corner we are in.

And you know my situation. Now, I have the financial responsibility for Reverend's mom.

We can help, but we have to do it together. I promise, I will do all I can for your family; however, I don't want any misunderstandings anymore.

I will continue to text Jessica and try to be with the children and honor your financial request. Rev said he would go over and pick the children up and do things with them.

Almost forgot—you should move your car. Ray doesn't care about your car or you. He has said as much, in his own way. If you write him, he will post it on his Facebook page. So please don't write him, for my sake.

OH! Rev Singleton wrote me a warm thank-you letter. He said he has texted you and is waiting to hear from you. Send him a note. I sent you his address.

In your letter, you mentioned no letters from family. Jonathan stopped by tonight and mentioned his children wrote to you Christmas day. Now you see how God has granted your request without my asking them. Jackie saw me writing you and decided to write you also, and I didn't ask her to.

God is all,
Mom

DECEMBER 28, 2013

LOVING YOU

Therefore if any man be in Christ, he is a new creature:
old things are passed away; behold, all things are become new.
II Corinthians 5:17 (KJV)

My Son,

I think my toe is getting better, since I tape it regularly. I made the decision to do this myself because the doctor's way doesn't allow you to bathe with their contraptions and bandages. You know I love bathing.

I received your pictures. This young man has lots of talent. When I visit, perhaps I will meet him. What is his name? Advocate work is difficult to promote. People like to search for information within the art, for example, the Mona Lisa. People don't know who she is smiling for. Is she smiling or what is she smiling about? Is she a man or a woman? Are her eyes following you? Is she a real person? So many questions. The artist is quite good at capturing one in the moment's presence. If he is to become exceptional, his characters must have more detail.

I told you Rev Evans called; he wants to see you. See you soon.

December 29, 2013

THINKING OF YOU

My Son,

Matthew 12:1–13

How are you? I am always happy to hear your voice.

I hope your visit with your dad, Jonathan, and little Jonathan went well.

When I went to jail protesting, in Vieques, Puerto Rico, the experience, perhaps, was really for this moment.

Something I wish to share with you: My visitors spoke of things I could not see because they had access to information on the outside that I had no access to. Not since the womb had I been in a bubble. I was no longer a part of the world of information. Everything I received was filtered and inspected. Fortunately, I was not in bad company. So most of the information I received was solely for my benefit.

You must begin to determine who is in this to save you. You must decide. I am coming to see you. I love you.

Mom

At that time Jesus went on the sabbath day through the corn; and his disciples were an hungred, and began to pluck the ears of corn, and to eat. But when the Pharisees saw it, they said unto him, Behold, thy disciples do that which is not lawful to do upon the sabbath day. But he said unto them, Have ye not

read what David did, when he was an hungred, and they that were with him; How he entered into the house of God, and did eat the shewbread, which was not lawful for him to eat, neither for them which were with him, but only for the priests. Or have ye not read in the law, how that on the sabbath days the priests in the temple profane the sabbath, and are blameless?

But I say unto you, That in this place is one greater than the temple.

But if ye had known what this meaneth, I will have mercy, and not sacrifice, ye would not have condemned the guiltless. For the Son of man is Lord even of the sabbath day.

And when he was departed thence, he went into their synagogue: And, behold, there was a man which had his hand withered. And they asked him, saying, Is it lawful to heal on the sabbath days? that they might accuse him. And he said unto them, What man shall there be among you, that shall have one sheep, and if it fall into a pit on the sabbath day, will he not lay hold on it, and lift it out? How much then is a man better than a sheep? Wherefore it is lawful to do well on the sabbath days.

Then saith he to the man, Stretch forth thine hand. And he stretched it forth; and it was restored whole, like as the other.

Matthew 12:1–13

THINKING OF YOU

If ye were of the world, the world would love his own:
but because ye are not of the world, but I have chosen you out
of the world, therefore the world hateth you.
John 15:19 (KJV)

My Son,

John 15:1–18

How are you?

I have called Connie; she is in Boston visiting her two grand-sons. She wanted to see you before returning to California, but I can't seem to pull this together any way. I am trying to see you on Friday, Saturday, and Sunday. I will make arrangements tomorrow. Call Allana to find out if I made it. Also, I went to Allene's today; she said, "Hello!"

Yusef is packing to leave the business. It is very emotional for him. I went to help him pack; he is very sad. I met the new owner; he may be younger than Yusef. He is the third generation in the Budweiser business. His dad started in the 1940s.

Good night. Love You.

✶

I am the true vine, and my Father is the husbandman. Every branch in me that beareth not fruit he taketh away: and every branch that beareth fruit, he purgeth it, that it may bring forth more fruit.

Now ye are clean through the word which I have spoken unto you. Abide in me, and I in you. As the branch cannot bear fruit of itself, except it abide in the vine; no more can ye, except ye abide in me.

I am the vine, ye are the branches: He that abideth in me, and I in him, the same bringeth forth much fruit: for without me ye can do nothing.

If a man abide not in me, he is cast forth as a branch, and is withered; and men gather them, and cast them into the fire, and they are burned.

If ye abide in me, and my words abide in you, ye shall ask what ye will, and it shall be done unto you.

Herein is my Father glorified, that ye bear much fruit; so shall ye be my disciples.

As the Father hath loved me, so have I loved you: continue ye in my love.

If ye keep my commandments, ye shall abide in my love; even as I have kept my Father's commandments, and abide in his love.

These things have I spoken unto you, that my joy might remain in you, and that your joy might be full.

This is my commandment, That ye love one another, as I have loved you.

Greater love hath no man than this, that a man lay down his life for his friends.

Ye are my friends, if ye do whatsoever I command you.

Henceforth I call you not servants; for the servant knoweth not what his lord doeth: but I have called you friends; for all things that I have heard of my Father I have made known unto you.

Ye have not chosen me, but I have chosen you, and ordained you, that ye should go and bring forth fruit, and that your fruit should remain: that whatsoever ye shall ask of the Father in my name, he may give it you.

These things I command you, that ye love one another.

If the world hate you, ye know that it hated me before it hated you.

John 15: 1–18 (KJV)

JANUARY 3, 2014

THINKING OF YOU

All things were made by him;
and without him was not any thing made that was made.
John 1:3 (KJV)

My Son,

Today Mr. Corry and I are traveling to North Carolina to see you. We didn't leave until 12:00. I was trying to wait for my bag from my flight to arrive; after it didn't arrive, we left for NC. The trip took us about 6 hours. We arrived at Wanda's house to receive instruction for the hotel and the directions to Butner. She insisted on taking us to dinner at a place across from the hotel. The restaurant was lovely. Mr. Corry's niece was married there, and he delivered some pictures he had taken of the wedding and the restaurant.

I stayed at the Hilton on or near Duke's campus. My stay was lovely. I was given one rate but charged another rate, higher, of course—will deal with that tomorrow.

God is good and good is God. Don't forget to pray.

Mom

YOU ARE ALWAYS ON MY MIND

My Son,

I don't know how I feel today, I know I must see you.

Mr. Corry and I have arrived too early. I am told I must wait until 8:30. The little girl in front of our car has a plastic bag she is carrying raised in the air with lots of change in it. I guess she is being escorted by her parents. Others are coming and forming a line at the counter outside of this facility.

Now I am closer to the door. A lady visiting someone passes me a piece of paper to fill out. It's a form of permission slip. I don't have my reading glasses, and I know it's going to take me all day to fill this form out.

Upon entering Butner facility, a nice man helped me because I forgot—couldn't remember for the life of me—your ID number. He looked you up and supplied it for me. I finished the form and took my place.

When you appeared, I was overjoyed to see you. I didn't mean to surprise you. I knew your father, who can't hold water, had told you my plans. I don't like surprises either. So forgive me for that.

LOVING YOU

But let patience have her perfect work,
that ye may be perfect and entire, wanting nothing.
James 1:4 (KJV)

My Son,

My visit with you and your new friends was delightful.

I am very happy to know you were not burdened with complaints. However, I didn't expect you to complain. That's just not the way you are.

This is not something I have ever wanted or even thought could have happened, but life is like a box of chocolates, you don't know what you have until you bite down into it.[1]

Now let me complain to you. What about that vending machine taking people's money at the prison? My, My, My! Of all places, at the prison. Rev's mother says, "People would do better if they knew better."

I think the concealed weapons law passed in Illinois . . . how sad we are as a country.

I have lived during the time when latching the screen door as you came into the house was enough. Then, the bars on the windows and doors became necessary. Then, the burglar alarm—now, before you leave home, don't forget your gun.

Where are we going as a nation and country?

At least we know a group of people who have given up on this nation and humanity . . . The Survivalist. I am beginning to think they know something, and that is very sad.

I love you so much. We have much to talk about.

January 6, 2014

LOVING YOU

But let patience have her perfect work,
that ye may be perfect and entire, wanting nothing.
James 1:4 (KJV)

My Son,

Don't forget to pray.

Yesterday, Sandra dropped by and brought the permission papers. She was on her way to exercise. The children picked up their Christmas gifts.

She said the family and some of her friends will visit you the King holiday weekend. I hope all goes well for you.

Jesse, is this supposed to be one of the better institutions?

Don't forget to feed your mind. Your diet of protein and reading is very, very important.

Your children are growing, and I was told they are doing well in school.

May God bless and keep you strong.

I will begin to pray my prosperity prayers for everyone who is good to you.

Remember, people who are not kind are in our lives for a purpose.

My love always,
Mom

LOVING YOU ALWAYS

James, a servant of God and of the Lord Jesus Christ, to the twelve tribes
which are scattered abroad, greeting. My brethren, count it all joy when
ye fall into divers temptations; Knowing this, that the trying of your faith
worketh patience. But let patience have her perfect work, that ye may be
perfect and entire, wanting nothing.
James 1:1–4 (KJV)

My Son,

Today, I went to the bank to get quarters. So upon my return, I won't have to go to the car wash in the middle of the night to retrieve quarters for the vending machine.

The machine, by the way, that stole my two dollars.

I am returning on Saturday because I need the assurance you are alright.

I am very concerned about your weight loss. Because of your surgery, your need for a high protein diet is essential, you know that. And I am sure the institution is aware of that also.

Institutional food is never the best. Maybe you can get a protein shake. Are they available?

I am going to call the lawyers and speak with my sister about this.

This is her field. I will get her to send you some information, and I will consult with Dr. Langdon, who knows about you and was responsible for your surgery.

Got lots to do.

Mom

THINKING OF YOU

My Son,

Don't forget to pray. Practice makes perfect.

There are two birds in my fireplace: one alive and one dead.

Never had this problem until the company that installed my new furnace did something to my chimney. They take their time responding to you when you don't owe them any money.

I placed water and bread in the fireplace; I hope the bird doesn't die before I can get someone to set it free. My mother said when birds come into the house, someone is going to die.

Interestingly, today, I saw a commercial on TV advertising building underground shelters on your property. This company will come out to your place to see if your property is in the appropriate location for the underground shelter, and they will build it for you.

Do you think someone knows something? More security, more security. What are we coming to?

When I visited you, I meant to get your opinion on the *Sister Wives* and the potential legalization of weed.

The places where drugs are legal like Amsterdam have their difficulties, that's for sure. But they don't have drive-bys. Zimmerman doesn't live there; there are no Bloods and Disciples. Their problems are problems, not race-laced problems. If their behavior is uncivil, it is not racially uncivil.

This is going to be a mess. Let's talk about this when we are together again. Until then.

I love you,
Mom

THINKING OF YOU

My Son,

Matthew 5:1–48

Due to the many cancelled planes, I am stuck at home until Connie catches her plane. The storm has been terrible; the ice has cracked my cement in the driveway, so that's another repair. No news today and that's a good thing.

This letter I found. This is the one I forgot to send. There is no need to waste paper, so I'll begin my new letter on this sheet.

I was in Amsterdam with Rev for a brief visit during an engagement that we had. I was made aware of the drug accessibility—you know, drugs are legal in Amsterdam. I have several friends who visited there at that time; I was not aware of their habit. They lost their lives there from drug overdoses. I really want to talk with you about America legalizing weed. They say now it is okay.

By the way, Mark Loveless said to me, "Mrs. J., you must call it cannabis now. It is not weed." I guess it's a class thing now. Poor people smoke and sell reefer and go to jail; upper-class people smoke and share it and have a party. Poor people are drunks, and go to jail; rich people are alcoholics and go to therapy. My question with the legalization of drugs, and the problems I have are, for one thing, I don't think it is healthy. Also, does this prevent you from being hired to fly a plane, drive trucks, supervise children, etc.? Can you engage in this and function and be employable in this society? My suggestion is, once you trick me into using this stuff, how have you isolated me further from society? What kind of employment culture—social and economic injustices—are we creating with this legalization of marijuana? What do you do with the people you have already scarred with imprisonment while you now permit others to do the very same things? There is no equal playing field. This is going to be a mess. Let's talk about this when we are together again.

❧

And seeing the multitudes, he went up into a mountain: and when he was set, his disciples came unto him:

And he opened his mouth, and taught them, saying,

Blessed are the poor in spirit: for theirs is the kingdom of heaven.

Blessed are they that mourn: for they shall be comforted.

Blessed are the meek: for they shall inherit the earth.

Blessed are they which do hunger and thirst after righteousness: for they shall be filled.

Blessed are the merciful: for they shall obtain mercy.

Blessed are the pure in heart: for they shall see God.

Blessed are the peacemakers: for they shall be called the children of God.

Blessed are they which are persecuted for righteousness' sake: for theirs is the kingdom of heaven.

Blessed are ye, when men shall revile you, and persecute you, and shall say all manner of evil against you falsely, for my sake.

Rejoice, and be exceeding glad: for great is your reward in heaven: for so persecuted they the prophets which were before you.

Ye are the salt of the earth: but if the salt have lost his savour, wherewith shall it be salted? it is thenceforth good for nothing, but to be cast out, and to be trodden under foot of men.

Ye are the light of the world. A city that is set on an hill cannot be hid.

Neither do men light a candle, and put it under a bushel, but on a candlestick; and it giveth light unto all that are in the house.

Let your light so shine before men, that they may see your good works, and glorify your Father which is in heaven.

Think not that I am come to destroy the law, or the prophets: I am not come to destroy, but to fulfill.

For verily I say unto you, Till heaven and earth pass, one jot or one tittle shall in no wise pass from the law, till all be fulfilled.

Whosoever therefore shall break one of these least commandments, and shall teach men so, he shall be called the least in the kingdom of heaven: but whosoever shall do and teach them, the same shall be called great in the kingdom of heaven.

For I say unto you, That except your righteousness shall exceed the righteousness of the scribes and Pharisees, ye shall in no case enter into the kingdom of heaven.

Ye have heard that it was said by them of old time, Thou shalt not kill; and whosoever shall kill shall be in danger of the judgment:

But I say unto you, That whosoever is angry with his brother without a cause shall be in danger of the judgment: and whosoever shall say to his brother, Raca, shall be in danger of the council: but whosoever shall say, Thou fool, shall be in danger of hell fire.

Therefore if thou bring thy gift to the altar, and there rememberest that thy brother hath ought against thee;

Leave there thy gift before the altar, and go thy way; first be reconciled to thy brother, and then come and offer thy gift.

Agree with thine adversary quickly, whiles thou art in the way with him; lest at any time the adversary deliver thee to the judge, and the judge deliver thee to the officer, and thou be cast into prison.

Verily I say unto thee, Thou shalt by no means come out thence, till thou hast paid the uttermost farthing.

Ye have heard that it was said by them of old time, Thou shalt not commit adultery:

But I say unto you, That whosoever looketh on a woman to lust after her hath committed adultery with her already in his heart.

And if thy right eye offend thee, pluck it out, and cast it from thee: for it is profitable for thee that one of thy members should perish, and not that thy whole body should be cast into hell.

And if thy right hand offend thee, cut it off, and cast it from thee: for it is profitable for thee that one of thy members should perish, and not that thy whole body should be cast into hell.

It hath been said, Whosoever shall put away his wife, let him give her a writing of divorcement:

But I say unto you, That whosoever shall put away his wife, saving for the cause of fornication, causeth her to commit adultery: and whosoever shall marry her that is divorced committeth adultery.

Again, ye have heard that it hath been said by them of old time, Thou shalt not forswear thyself, but shalt perform unto the Lord thine oaths:

But I say unto you, Swear not at all; neither by heaven; for it is God's throne:

Nor by the earth; for it is his footstool: neither by Jerusalem; for it is the city of the great King.

Neither shalt thou swear by thy head, because thou canst not make one hair white or black.

But let your communication be, Yea, yea; Nay, nay: for whatsoever is more than these cometh of evil.

Ye have heard that it hath been said, An eye for an eye, and a tooth for a tooth:

But I say unto you, That ye resist not evil: but whosoever shall smite thee on thy right cheek, turn to him the other also.

And if any man will sue thee at the law, and take away thy coat, let him have thy cloak also.

And whosoever shall compel thee to go a mile, go with him twain.

Give to him that asketh thee, and from him that would borrow of thee turn not thou away.

Ye have heard that it hath been said, Thou shalt love thy neighbour, and hate thine enemy.

But I say unto you, Love your enemies, bless them that curse you, do good to them that hate you, and pray for them which despitefully use you, and persecute you;

That ye may be the children of your Father which is in heaven: for he maketh his sun to rise on the evil and on the good, and sendeth rain on the just and on the unjust.

For if ye love them which love you, what reward have ye? do not even the publicans the same?

And if ye salute your brethren only, what do ye more than others? do not even the publicans so?

Be ye therefore perfect, even as your Father which is in heaven is perfect.

Matthew 5:1–48 (KJV)

January 10, 2014

LOVING YOU

James, a servant of God and of the Lord Jesus Christ, to the twelve tribes which are scattered abroad, greeting. My brethren, count it all joy when ye fall into divers temptations; Knowing this, that the trying of your faith worketh patience. But let patience have her perfect work, that ye may be perfect and entire, wanting nothing.

James 1:1–4 (KJV)

My Son,

My day began very early. Mr. Corry is going to a conference; I must take him to the airport.

Dara and I had planned to drive to North Carolina today and spend the night; but I am too tired, and we will travel early tomorrow morning. So tonight, I will fill the gas tank, pick up some fruit, and go to bed early for tomorrow morning. I hope the rain stops so we will have a beautiful sky tomorrow. Going in early.

Love,
Mom

P.S. The painter stopped by, said, "Hello." So did Ms. Berna and Jo Bee.

THINKING OF YOU

My Son,

Psalms 24

We left for NC at 4:00 on the dot. I had to return home . . . forgot my bag. Can you believe that?

Our drive all—all—the way to NC was a nightmare. It stormed all the way here, and it was as black as the pit, from pole to pole.

After Petersburg, I had to pull over and ask Dara to drive. I couldn't see anymore.

At about 8:00, when we were arriving in Durham, there wasn't any visibility. We never saw the sun.

We went directly to the hotel, then directly to see you.

I did so enjoy my visit with you.

I'll do everything to give the art project as much exposure as possible.

Good luck,

Mom

A Psalm of David

The earth is the Lord's, and the fulness thereof; the world, and they that dwell therein.

For he hath founded it upon the seas, and established it upon the floods.

Who shall ascend into the hill of the Lord? or who shall stand in his holy place?

He that hath clean hands, and a pure heart; who hath not lifted up his soul unto vanity, nor sworn deceitfully.

He shall receive the blessing from the Lord, and righteousness from the God of his salvation.

This is the generation of them that seek him, that seek thy face, O Jacob. Selah.

Lift up your heads, O ye gates; and be ye lift up, ye everlasting doors; and the King of glory shall come in.

Who is this King of glory? The Lord strong and mighty, the Lord mighty in battle.

Lift up your heads, O ye gates; even lift them up, ye everlasting doors; and the King of glory shall come in.

Who is this King of glory? The Lord of hosts, he is the King of glory. Selah.

Psalms 24 (KJV)

January 12, 2014

THINKING OF YOU

James, a servant of God and of the Lord Jesus Christ, to the twelve tribes which are scattered abroad, greeting. My brethren, count it all joy when ye fall into divers temptations; Knowing this, that the trying of your faith worketh patience. But let patience have her perfect work, that ye may be perfect and entire, wanting nothing.
James 1:1–4 (KJV)

My Son,

My trip back to Washington was very easy. Dara is an excellent driver, I've discovered. I had a lot of meditation time with you, Jesse, while driving. Please take care of yourself.

I am in Washington, DC and don't have access to my research material. I believe it was Richard Lovelace who said: "Walls do not a prison make, Nor iron bars a cage."[1]

Please don't become a prisoner. Mandela didn't, King didn't, and many others didn't. I love you.

Mom

LOVING YOU ALWAYS

And as ye would that men should do to you,
do ye also to them likewise.
Luke 6:31 (KJV)

My Son,

Don't forget to pray.

I spoke with Santita. She has been with your doctors. They have created some new vitamins necessary for your health.

I am going to reach out to Dr. Langdon for help for you. You should take your surgery very seriously.

You are what you eat. Remember, the body is alive.

Love you all the time,
Mom

January 14, 2014

LOVING YOU

My Son,

    Matthew 5:1–48

    Before I forget, Jim Beam liquor was bought by China recently.

    Now, my car was towed today. I have to go downtown to deny the two tickets.

    CK called; she said she is coming down to see you.

Must go to bed,
Mom

And seeing the multitudes, he went up into a mountain: and when he was set, his disciples came unto him:

    And he opened his mouth, and taught them, saying,

    Blessed are the poor in spirit: for theirs is the kingdom of heaven.

    Blessed are they that mourn: for they shall be comforted.

    Blessed are the meek: for they shall inherit the earth.

    Blessed are they which do hunger and thirst after righteousness: for they shall be filled.

    Blessed are the merciful: for they shall obtain mercy.

    Blessed are the pure in heart: for they shall see God.

    Blessed are the peacemakers: for they shall be called the children of God.

    Blessed are they which are persecuted for righteousness' sake: for theirs is the kingdom of heaven.

Blessed are ye, when men shall revile you, and persecute you, and shall say all manner of evil against you falsely, for my sake.

Rejoice, and be exceeding glad: for great is your reward in heaven: for so persecuted they the prophets which were before you.

Ye are the salt of the earth: but if the salt have lost his savour, wherewith shall it be salted? it is thenceforth good for nothing, but to be cast out, and to be trodden under foot of men.

Ye are the light of the world. A city that is set on an hill cannot be hid.

Neither do men light a candle, and put it under a bushel, but on a candlestick; and it giveth light unto all that are in the house.

Let your light so shine before men, that they may see your good works, and glorify your Father which is in heaven.

Think not that I am come to destroy the law, or the prophets: I am not come to destroy, but to fulfill.

For verily I say unto you, Till heaven and earth pass, one jot or one tittle shall in no wise pass from the law, till all be fulfilled.

Whosoever therefore shall break one of these least commandments, and shall teach men so, he shall be called the least in the kingdom of heaven: but whosoever shall do and teach them, the same shall be called great in the kingdom of heaven.

For I say unto you, That except your righteousness shall exceed the righteousness of the scribes and Pharisees, ye shall in no case enter into the kingdom of heaven.

Ye have heard that it was said by them of old time, Thou shalt not kill; and whosoever shall kill shall be in danger of the judgment:

But I say unto you, That whosoever is angry with his brother without a cause shall be in danger of the judgment: and whosoever shall say to his brother, Raca, shall be in danger of the council: but whosoever shall say, Thou fool, shall be in danger of hell fire.

Therefore if thou bring thy gift to the altar, and there rememberest that thy brother hath ought against thee;

Leave there thy gift before the altar, and go thy way; first be reconciled to thy brother, and then come and offer thy gift.

Agree with thine adversary quickly, whiles thou art in the way with him; lest at any time the adversary deliver thee to the judge, and the judge deliver thee to the officer, and thou be cast into prison.

Verily I say unto thee, Thou shalt by no means come out thence, till thou hast paid the uttermost farthing.

Ye have heard that it was said by them of old time, Thou shalt not commit adultery:

But I say unto you, That whosoever looketh on a woman to lust after her hath committed adultery with her already in his heart.

And if thy right eye offend thee, pluck it out, and cast it from thee: for it is profitable for thee that one of thy members should perish, and not that thy whole body should be cast into hell.

And if thy right hand offend thee, cut it off, and cast it from thee: for it is profitable for thee that one of thy members should perish, and not that thy whole body should be cast into hell.

It hath been said, Whosoever shall put away his wife, let him give her a writing of divorcement:

But I say unto you, That whosoever shall put away his wife, saving for the cause of fornication, causeth her to commit adultery: and whosoever shall marry her that is divorced committeth adultery.

Again, ye have heard that it hath been said by them of old time, Thou shalt not forswear thyself, but shalt perform unto the Lord thine oaths:

But I say unto you, Swear not at all; neither by heaven; for it is God's throne:

Nor by the earth; for it is his footstool: neither by Jerusalem; for it is the city of the great King.

Neither shalt thou swear by thy head, because thou canst not make one hair white or black.

But let your communication be, Yea, yea; Nay, nay: for whatsoever is more than these cometh of evil.

Ye have heard that it hath been said, An eye for an eye, and a tooth for a tooth:

But I say unto you, That ye resist not evil: but whosoever shall smite thee on thy right cheek, turn to him the other also.

And if any man will sue thee at the law, and take away thy coat, let him have thy cloak also.

And whosoever shall compel thee to go a mile, go with him twain.

Give to him that asketh thee, and from him that would borrow of thee turn not thou away.

Ye have heard that it hath been said, Thou shalt love thy neighbour, and hate thine enemy.

But I say unto you, Love your enemies, bless them that curse you, do good to them that hate you, and pray for them which despitefully use you, and persecute you;

That ye may be the children of your Father which is in heaven: for he maketh his sun to rise on the evil and on the good, and sendeth rain on the just and on the unjust.

For if ye love them which love you, what reward have ye? do not even the publicans the same?

And if ye salute your brethren only, what do ye more than others? do not even the publicans so?

Be ye therefore perfect, even as your Father which is in heaven is perfect.

Matthew 5:1–48 (KJV)

January 15, 2014

LOVING YOU

Who hath ears to hear, let him hear. And the disciples came, and said unto him, Why speakest thou unto them in parables? He answered and said unto them, Because it is given unto you to know the mysteries of the kingdom of heaven, but to them it is not given.
Matthew 13:9–11 (KJV)

My Son,

Some guys robbed an armored car and hid under Ray's house. The four men were under his house hiding; they were apprehended. I saw Ray describing the event on TV.

Love you,
Mom

I LOVE YOU

My Son,

Don't forget to pray.

I am so sorry I have had to break my promise of writing to you every day. I will begin to write you more often as soon as my mother is settled.

I am the only one handling this stroke Mom had. She is a very difficult patient. All the things that made her strong are now working against her and weakening her.

I have to cook her food and take it to her or she will not eat. My day is very complicated with all I have to do already.

You should call me, so I will know what I am doing about the mail I am to send. Your instructions were not clear.

God Is Good,
Mom

P.S.: I want to write you about the miracle of her stroke. She laid on a cold floor from 7:00 p.m. to 10:00 a.m.

LOVING YOU ALL THE TIME

My Son,

Matthew 6:8–14

OH, how hurt I am for not keeping my promise to you.

I love you as much as my mom loves me, yet I have had to make a choice as to what to do first.

I could have written you little meaningless notes or wait until I am not too tired to tell you of my recent experience.

I didn't want to send you empty thoughts during this period. I didn't want to do that.

January 15th, I was preparing a meal for your dad; at about 6:30 I received a call from one of mom's new young friends, Kim. She said, "Mrs. J, call your mom. I cannot reach her. I was speaking with her and her voice slurred." I began calling her at about 7:00 or 7:15, and the line was busy.

I called Connie, and had to convince her to get her friends to go by mom's house to check on her. Connie's classmate went to the house about 9:00 p.m., knocking on all her doors . . . no response.

I called AT&T, Verizon, and 911, asking them to interrupt her phone and ask her to call me. I have done this in the past. They all said they don't do that anymore. How about that!

Yet, they can eavesdrop on people—and can't help you in a crisis. I pleaded with them to help me. "We cannot help you," they all said. I told them my mother's aged 86; all this was in vain.

I don't drive so well at night anymore. So all I could do was wait until morning.

I called Dara, who had just returned with me from Butner on Sunday. But she agreed to drive down to Virginia with me.

On the way to Hampton, while we were just outside of Richmond, Dara decided to call Grandma again. Just as she dialed, there was a hang up of her phone. Dara said, "What a relief, Gertie just hung up the phone. She is alright." I asked her to call again. "This is Officer Coleman. Is this Mrs. Brown's daughter from Washington, DC?" "Yes," I replied, "yes." He said he had to knock the door in to gain entry. She had been on the cold floor all night long, from 6:30 p.m. until 10:00 a.m. She had a large cut over her left eye. And her eye was three times its normal size.

Her eye healed within 10 days, and she didn't get a black eye. Miracle. My next letter will be about all the miracles I've experienced these past weeks and the lessons I've learned.

Mom's first hospital stay was not a nice stay.

As you well know, mom is a retired hospital worker. Today she refuses to eat food prepared for the public, and she would not eat food in the hospital. So, I have had to bring food to the hospital for her to eat; it is taxing. I prepare a big lunch for her.

One particular day, I arrived late . . . about 1:00 p.m. There my mother was—soaking wet, lying in waste. I can't tell you how angry and upset I was.

I promised myself I would not allow that to happen again.

I asked for help and told them I only wanted their assistance as I cleaned her myself. After I cleaned her, I told them, "If this was your mother, I would have cleaned your mother, just as I did for my mother, who is helpless."

How sad I am for who we have become as a people.

Jesse, things happen and life is never the same, whether LeMans, St. Albans, Aggie Pride, Congress, or Butner.

My life is not the same.

I love life. How exciting it is.

I will write you next time about the lessons I've learned. And the miracles I saw.

I am sure even you and some of the people are a part of miracles. You just don't recognize them because you don't give God a chance.

I love you with all my heart,
Mom

The Lord's Prayer

Be not ye therefore like unto them: for your Father knoweth what things ye have need of, before ye ask him.

After this manner therefore pray ye:

Our Father which art in heaven, Hallowed be thy name. Thy kingdom come.

Thy will be done in earth, as it is in heaven.

Give us this day our daily bread.

And forgive us our debts, as we forgive our debtors.

And lead us not into temptation, but deliver us from evil: For thine is the kingdom, and the power, and the glory, for ever. Amen.

For if ye forgive men their trespasses, your heavenly Father will also forgive you.

Matthew 6:8–14 (KJV)

THINKING OF YOU

My Son,

Psalm 62

Today while sitting by the door of my mother's bed, who should pass in a wheelchair? None other than one of the loves of my life: Marion Barry.

I had promised to braid mom's hair, and she must have sensed my anxiousness to talk with Mayor Barry.

She gets so jealous when I spend time with anyone but her.

She talks about you all time, Jesse. When you return, she wants you to promise her you will come back to work in the community in some way.

Now, back to Mayor Marion Barry. Mom watches the City Council meetings every day just to see Marion; yet she is very jealous of my visits with him during his hospital stay, unless she is next door in his room with me. And then, I can't get a word in the conversation.

So today I got her straight. I told her he is one of my heroes, and I can never forget the courage and support he gave us when your dad ran for president. Now let people tell it, many say they supported Rev's effort when he ran for president. You know that is not true. I remember when Mayor Hatcher volunteered to chair Rev's campaign for president, and I don't know what happened to him, because we didn't see him until the campaign nearly ended. He had the biggest fight with Marion Barry because he felt he should introduce Rev the night of the Democratic Convention. I must note

Hatcher kept the title of Chair because Rev thought it would be disruptive to remove him from that position.

Marion took the floor at our campaign staff meeting and said to Mayor Hatcher and all present, "I am going to do the introduction of Rev because I have earned it, and there is no more to be said about the matter." And nothing else was said.

Also Jesse, it was Marion who opened the doors of Washington, DC Convention Center for Rev to make his campaign announcement. He supported Rev's run for shadow Senator also.

While visiting Marion, he told me he had just finished his autobiography. As we talked, I asked him will this be included in the book. He said, "No," he had forgotten to include most of the things we discussed.

Jesse, he is a won-der-ful person. He asked me how are you doing when I first went in the room. I should have told you in the beginning. Before I could answer, he said, "Tell him, 'Don't count the days. Just relax and do the time,'" and he began sharing with me some of his experiences while in prison.

He shared at length details of how a few guards went out of their way to harass him, make his stay more difficult, and really break his spirit.

I became quite sad to know of the harassment he experienced while in jail. And it is hard to believe this man, who has given so much to people, could be ridiculed and unappreciated by one given superficial power to oppress someone God has blessed.

Marion has given over 300,000 young people of Washington, DC jobs. He single-handedly created Bob Johnson of BET and Cathy Hughes of TV One station, and brought almost as many Blacks into the middle-class as your dad.

Ingratitude is an act of violence.

But ain't God something. Then the God Factor happened. Who would have thought that Marion, after going to jail, would become

Mayor again . . . only to meet one of the men who harassed him, and give him a job. God is good.

I love you so much,
Mom

✧

A Psalm of David

Truly my soul waiteth upon God: from him cometh my salvation.

He only is my rock and my salvation; he is my defence; I shall not be greatly moved.

How long will ye imagine mischief against a man? ye shall be slain all of you: as a bowing wall shall ye be, and as a tottering fence.

They only consult to cast him down from his excellency: they delight in lies: they bless with their mouth, but they curse inwardly. Selah.

My soul, wait thou only upon God; for my expectation is from him.

He only is my rock and my salvation: he is my defence; I shall not be moved.

In God is my salvation and my glory: the rock of my strength, and my refuge, is in God.

Trust in him at all times; ye people, pour out your heart before him: God is a refuge for us. Selah.

Surely men of low degree are vanity, and men of high degree are a lie: to be laid in the balance, they are altogether lighter than vanity.

Trust not in oppression, and become not vain in robbery: if riches increase, set not your heart upon them.

God hath spoken once; twice have I heard this; that power belongeth unto God.

Also unto thee, O Lord, belongeth mercy: for thou renderest to every man according to his work.

Psalm 63 (KJV)

THINKING OF YOU

My Son,

Psalms 63

Don't forget to pray; it works.

Today, we are making plans to move Mom to another facility. I must pack her things from the house. Also, she won't eat if I don't prepare the food. I love her, but she is a handful.

Connie is trying to downsize her house.

I love you,
Mom

P.S. It was Courtney who told me about this place. The place was Sibley Memorial Hospital Renaissance Rehabilitation Center. One of the most prestigious places in the DC area, and I mean the finest facility.

Thank you.

A Psalm of David, when he was in the wilderness of Judah

O God, thou art my God; early will I seek thee: my soul thirsteth for thee, my flesh longeth for thee in a dry and thirsty land, where no water is;

To see thy power and thy glory, so as I have seen thee in the sanctuary. Because thy lovingkindness is better than life, my lips shall praise thee. Thus will I bless thee while I live: I will lift up my hands in thy name.

My soul shall be satisfied as with marrow and fatness; and my mouth shall praise thee with joyful lips:

When I remember thee upon my bed, and meditate on thee in the night watches.

Because thou hast been my help, therefore in the shadow of thy wings will I rejoice.

My soul followeth hard after thee: thy right hand upholdeth me.

But those that seek my soul, to destroy it, shall go into the lower parts of the earth.

They shall fall by the sword: they shall be a portion for foxes.

But the king shall rejoice in God; every one that sweareth by him shall glory: but the mouth of them that speak lies shall be stopped.

Psalms 63 (KJV)

THINKING OF YOU

My Son,

Psalms 63

Today I took mom to Sibley Rehab. I mean the ambulance did. I observed the rumors to be true. This is a great facility. Mom was there for perhaps 3–4 weeks; I don't know, specifically, how long. She was there for approximately 4 weeks. Jesse, she complained E-V-E-R-Y day. This facility was so patient with her. The family exit meeting hurt me deeply. I was told Mom can never live alone. She is not able to make decisions on her own anymore. She is so determined to be so-called independent again (as if she ever was) that she lies about getting up at night and going to the bathroom. The strong will that gave her a full life can now destroy her. I love her so much.

Mom talks about you all the time. The old days.

P.S. And most of all, I have had the money order. How do I fill it out? I will visit you maybe on the 14th or 15th.

Love,

Mom

A Psalm of David, when he was in the wilderness of Judah

O God, thou art my God; early will I seek thee: my soul thirsteth for thee, my flesh longeth for thee in a dry and thirsty land, where no water is;

To see thy power and thy glory, so as I have seen thee in the sanctuary.

Because thy lovingkindness is better than life, my lips shall praise thee.

Thus will I bless thee while I live: I will lift up my hands in thy name.

My soul shall be satisfied as with marrow and fatness; and my mouth shall praise thee with joyful lips:

When I remember thee upon my bed, and meditate on thee in the night watches.

Because thou hast been my help, therefore in the shadow of thy wings will I rejoice.

My soul followeth hard after thee: thy right hand upholdeth me.

But those that seek my soul, to destroy it, shall go into the lower parts of the earth.

They shall fall by the sword: they shall be a portion for foxes.

But the king shall rejoice in God; every one that sweareth by him shall glory: but the mouth of them that speak lies shall be stopped.

Psalms 63 (KJV)

THINKING OF YOU

My Son,

    Psalms 64—please read

    Prayer works.

    Mom has the best insurance in the world. She has Medicare, Blue Cross, and something called Tricare, which can pay for a stay in a top care institution for months, for almost nothing, in a private room. Unbelievable. It includes medicine. The only thing her insurance doesn't pay for is her ride to Washington, DC, from Hampton, VA, and the ride to the new hospital. Their insurance even paid for Granddaddy Brown's helicopter ride to the hospital. I guess that's because of the wars he was in.

    Your dad and I will just have to drop dead because we cannot afford to be sick in the USA.

I love you,
Mom

A Psalm of David

Hear my voice, O God, in my prayer: preserve my life from fear of the enemy.

    Hide me from the secret counsel of the wicked; from the insurrection of the workers of iniquity:

Who whet their tongue like a sword, and bend their bows to shoot their arrows, even bitter words:

That they may shoot in secret at the perfect: suddenly do they shoot at him, and fear not.

They encourage themselves in an evil manner: they commune of laying snares privily; they say, Who shall see them?

They search out iniquities; they accomplish a diligent search: both the inward thought of every one of them, and the heart, is deep.

But God shall shoot at them with an arrow; suddenly shall they be wounded.

So they shall make their own tongue to fall upon themselves: all that see them shall flee away.

And all men shall fear, and shall declare the work of God; for they shall wisely consider of his doing.

The righteous shall be glad in the Lord, and shall trust in him; and all the upright in heart shall glory.

Psalms 64 (KJV)

THINKING OF YOU

My brethren, count it all joy when ye fall into divers temptations; Knowing this, that the trying of your faith worketh patience. But let patience have her perfect work, that ye may be perfect and entire, wanting nothing.
James 1:2–4 (KJV)

My Son,

As always don't forget to pray.

I've just returned from Hampton, VA, this morning. I went to wrap and pack Mom's collection of porcelain. I'll go back in a few days to try and pack some of her lamps.

Thank God for my running buddy, Mr. Corry. He came with me because he is my best friend. He stayed in Mom's house with me and my sister Connie. If Mom knew he had spent the night in her house, she would have died. You know how she is about company.

You can never tell Mom because she would have a fit. She wants no one in her house. There is so much there in disrepair because she won't let anyone in to help her. She has so much stored in the garage; the mice are having a field day.

This is just a little note to get back into the routine of writing you every day.

I've got to go to the hospital now, so I've written you early during the day.

Mom is very depressed.

Rev has a sleeping problem. He is using some kind of machine to help him.

Chuck is not doing well at all. He is in and out of the hospital. And you know he is really suffering.

Got to go see Mom.

I love you,
Mom

LOVING YOU SO MUCH

My brethren, count it all joy when ye fall into divers temptations; Knowing this, that the trying of your faith worketh patience. But let patience have her perfect work, that ye may be perfect and entire, wanting nothing.
James 1:2–4 (KJV)

My Son,

Prayer works!

It is morning, and a beautiful layer of snow is on the ground.

I love the snow and every season.

God's world is so very beautiful.

Courtney comes to see my mother every day almost. She always brings something for her. I have told her repeatedly to stop bringing things. But she insists. I think she feels we will not accept her if she doesn't bring something. It hurts to know she may feel that way because she is quite a lovely person.

I love her visits and her sense of family and friendship. I am grateful for her presence in Mom's and my life.

Mom's purpose for going to Virginia this time was to demand that her neighbor and best friend, Ms. Brinkley, tell her doctor off for letting her have a stroke. Mom said Ms. Brinkley eats the proper foods and exercised by playing golf. "She does everything right," she said.

Now, Ms. Brinkley is 91 years old, and my mom thinks the stroke was the fault of the doctor.

Well, guess what? Mom arrived in Hampton on Monday night.

Tuesday night, before she could see her friend Ms. Brinkley, she had her own stroke. Now Mom doesn't understand how or why she has had a stroke.

It's the God Factor, Jesse.

Remember the book "Killa" Mitch the Barber said he was going to write? He said he had to write the book, but he already had the title for it: *Shut Up, MF! You May Be Next.*

THINKING OF YOU

My Son,

Don't forget to pray.

Mom is doing okay. The forecast today is for 12 inches of snow this evening, so I am writing you early. Things go crazy here in Washington.

Mom still wants me to bring her food. I've told her time and time again, because of her medicines, it is best to eat the food the hospital prepares for her. As usual, she doesn't listen.

Today, I have decided to stop talking with Mom's doctors alone, trying to spare her feelings of some of her new realities. Now I am going to insist that she be present when we discuss her. The stroke has left her somewhat confused.

You know she has always exaggerated her life. Now she is doing it to hide the things she can't do.

First, she wouldn't admit she had a stroke. She kept saying she simply fell and hit her head.

It has taken the doctors 3 weeks to make her say she had a stroke.

We are still having trouble making her eat the hospital food. She wants me to bring her food and wash her clothes. The hospital is very far away, and it takes me 45 minutes to get there, and that's without heavy traffic. I make the trip every day, ofttimes twice a day.

I am planning to take her back to Chicago when she is stronger.

I am going to order you some books and send them to you next week.

I had hoped to visit you this weekend . . . maybe for a day if Mr. Corry visits his niece in Durham. But the snow may create a problem.

Don't forget to read.

Love you always,
Mom

FEBRUARY 12, 2014

LOVING YOU MORE EACH DAY

My brethren, count it all joy when ye fall into divers temptations; Knowing this, that the trying of your faith worketh patience. But let patience have her perfect work, that ye may be perfect and entire, wanting nothing.
James 1:2–4(KJV)

My Son,

I've just returned from the hospital with Connie.

Mom was glad to see her. Mom has no idea that Connie has been in Virginia getting rid of things in the garage and she had to remove tons of garbage.

There was an old woman in our neighborhood when we were growing up. Her name was Mrs. Wind. Mom is just like her—almost. She had the junkiest house and yard, as well as a bunch of cats that followed her. The difference between Mrs. Wind and Mom is that Mom is afraid of cats.

Connie shredded 22 bags of paper. It's unbelievable. What is remarkable is that there are no signs of mice in her place. What a relief.

I have asked Mom to let us clean the place. She keeps saying, "Just wait until I am up again." So today, I confronted her. "Mom," I asked, "do you really think you are going to be able to go through all these things, boxes, and dresser drawers?" She didn't answer. I said, "Let me put it this way. Mom, do you think I will ever be a majorette, again?" "No, you can just forget that!" she said. "Now, just you think about yourself going up and down the stairs, as you did before."

[137]

Jesse, Mom is a little mean too. Connie says Mom has dementia; I refuse to believe that.

Please don't tell this to Sandy. I don't want to hear this again.

Don't forget to pray.

Love you much,
Mom

February 13, 2014

LOVING YOU

For ye have the poor with you always, and whensoever ye will ye may do them good: but me ye have not always. She hath done what she could: she is come aforehand to anoint my body to the burying. Verily I say unto you, Wheresoever this gospel shall be preached throughout the whole world, this also that she hath done shall be spoken of for a memorial of her.
Mark 14:7–9 (KJV)

My Son,

Today Connie and I are stuck in the house. Mr. Corry sent his son over to clean the driveway this morning. But later, the snow is back again. I am sure all recorded records for snow in America have been broken this year. How are you? I hope you are eating better. Remember you are what you eat and think.

People always ask about you, Jesse. Please read about the life of Paul. Don't let anyone break your spirit.

It's late; I am tired. Will write more tomorrow.

Love,
Mom

LOVING YOU EVERY DAY

My Son,

Put on the full armor of God.

Rev sent me some flowers for Valentine's Day. I took them to Mom.

Dara went with me to the hospital. Jesse, Dara is a very nice person. She loves fun, clothes, people, and her husband. When we arrived, Courtney was there. I told her I was going to tell you that she was killing Gertie with all the sugar she brings her.

Kim comes to see Gertie also. You don't know her. She is a GS 15 and about 43 or something, and a very nice, responsible young lady. We disagree on many political issues; she is very conservative. For example, she believes America has to do something harsh to Snowden to make an example of him. I told her we cannot shock and awe people. We are going to have to find new solutions to win good favor.

Gertie is doing fine. She can stand now. She can walk with a walker pretty good. And, she is getting stronger. Praise the Lord. The doctor at the last hospital told me to take her home.

Yusef and I fought bitterly over my decision to not bring her home. He thought I didn't want to take care of her, which is a long way from the truth.

The same doctor told me he likes to get stroke victims on the third day of the stroke because the sooner the therapy begins, the better the results.

It took twelve days or more to regulate Mom's heartbeat, cholesterol, and other problems. And since she has good, good insurance, why not get the best they had to offer . . . if it increases her chances for a better life?

I am very happy with the results of my decision. Mom can walk again, and her spirit is back.

Mom will be 87 on March 7th. She wants me to stop coming to see her and come to see you, so she can know how you are doing. She loves you more than the other children, you know that. I don't think that is fair, but that's the way she is. By the way, when I tried to help her, she said, "Stop, you are hurting me." Each time, these white people ask her to do something, she never complains.

Love always,
Mom

P.S. Because of my dispute with Yusef, he has stopped speaking to me for a while. He always does this. Just want you to know we don't always get along.

🌱

Put on the whole armour of God, that ye may be able to stand against the wiles of the devil. For we wrestle not against flesh and blood, but against principalities, against powers, against the rulers of the darkness of this world, against spiritual wickedness in high places. Wherefore take unto you the whole armour of God, that ye may be able to withstand in the evil day, and having done all, to stand. Stand therefore, having your loins girt about with truth, and having on the breastplate of righteousness; And your feet shod with the preparation of the gospel of peace;

Above all, taking the shield of faith, wherewith ye shall be able to quench all the fiery darts of the wicked. And take the helmet of salvation, and the sword of the Spirit, which is the word of God: Praying always with all prayer and supplication in the Spirit, and watching thereunto with all perseverance and supplication for all saints.

Ephesians 6:11–18 (KJV)

FEBRUARY 15, 2014

LOVING YOU ALWAYS

My Son,

Don't forget to pray! Put on the full armor of God.

I hope to see you this weekend, if all goes well.

Today I spent the entire day visiting every Walmart in the area trying to find (for Mom) the elastic bottom jogging pants. I have not been able to find (for her therapy session) a size large Fruit of the Loom jogging pants here in Washington, DC or Maryland. I am on my way to the hospital, and I am tired.

Mr. Corry has driven me every day since she has been ill. Even when he travels for personal purposes, he searches for things to make Mom comfortable. And I am grateful.

Will write you more the next time.

I love you so much,
Mom

ψ

Put on the whole armour of God, that ye may be able to stand against the wiles of the devil. For we wrestle not against flesh and blood, but against principalities, against powers, against the rulers of the darkness of this world, against spiritual wickedness in high places. Wherefore take unto you the whole armour of God, that ye may be able to withstand in the evil day, and having done all, to stand. Stand therefore, having your loins girt about with truth, and having on the breastplate of righteousness; And your feet shod with the preparation of the gospel of peace; Above all, taking the shield of faith, wherewith ye shall be able to quench all the fiery darts of the wicked. And take the helmet of salvation, and the sword of the Spirit, which is the word of God: Praying always with all prayer and supplication in the Spirit, and watching thereunto with all perseverance and supplication for all saints.

Ephesians 6:11–18 (KJV)

FEBRUARY 16, 2014

LOVING YOU ALWAYS

James, a servant of God and of the Lord Jesus Christ,
to the twelve tribes which are scattered abroad, greeting.
My brethren, count it all joy when ye fall into divers temptations; Knowing
this, that the trying of your faith worketh patience.
James 1–1:3 (KJV)

My Son,

You are always on my mind. How are you?

Today, Mr. Corry and I searched once more for Mom's jogging pants. Now I mean it this time, I am not searching any more for the sweatpants (Fruit of the Loom) with the elastic at the legs. Mom is so specific, just as she won't wear some of the other jogging suits I have already bought for her.

Mom has yet to have a reality check; slowly, I am having mine. She has been told repeatedly she can never live alone; she will need assistance to walk from now on. You know Mom doesn't trust people, so who can I get to help her? I mean, no one does she trust, including me or Connie—her only two daughters.

Yusef keeps asking the question to Mom, "What have you learned from this experience?" She said (and I quote), "I should have kept my money!?" I think she has lost her mind.

Most people say, "Thank you, Lord for waking me up this morning, clothed in my right mind." And they say, "Thank you Dear Lord, for not making my bed my cooling board." Tradition. By that I mean throughout Black history, that is the saying of our people, and my sentiment; but my Mom, I sometimes wonder.

What have I learned? I am so grateful for this period of growth.

I love you so much,
Mom

FEBRUARY 17, 2014

THINKING OF YOU

*James, a servant of God and of the Lord Jesus Christ, to the twelve tribes
which are scattered abroad, greeting.
My brethren, count it all joy when ye fall into divers temptations; Knowing
this, that the trying of your faith worketh patience.*
James 1–1:3 (KJV)

My Son,

How are you? Don't forget to pray always.

The doctors have said they are now in the process of discharging Mom from the hospital. So this is it, sometime next week. So I am very busy now.

I don't want to bring her home to sit in front of a TV all day. Nor do I want to send her to a senior center to play Bingo or be babysat. She wants to come home, and you know that she wants to be with me. So, I'll be in the same situation as Allene. I never thought I would be in this situation. I have a big problem. I must find her someone close who can be with her, or I don't know. I must decide alone. Remember when I had every solution for Allene as she cared for her mother alone? Now, I am walking in those shoes.

UNDATED #3

My Son,

Don't forget to pray.

After I wrote you yesterday, I gave some thought to my dilemma—what I should do with Mom.

I had every solution for Allene and her mom; now I am faced with the same problem. A lesson learned. Be careful as you misunderstand things or other people and their issues because God will give you a first-hand opportunity for understanding. Also, be careful how you engage others' adversities with all the answers. God will bring you to the same problem.

Remember the book "Killa" Mitch, Rev's barber, said he was going to write? He said he had to write this book because he already had the title for it. The title was *Shut Up, MF! You May Be Next.* And here I am.

Got to go. Love you from your heart to your toe.

I love you,
Mom

FEBRUARY 18, 2014

LOVING YOU

James, a servant of God and of the Lord Jesus Christ, to the twelve tribes
which are scattered abroad, greeting.
My brethren, count it all joy when ye fall into divers temptations; Knowing
this, that the trying of your faith worketh patience.
James 1–1:3 (KJV)

My Son,

I think of you always. Don't forget to pray.

Today, I am cleaning the basement. I didn't go to the hospital today, and boy do I feel guilty.

Tomorrow I will stop at the hospital to see her doctor and to seek help for myself. I must determine where we go from here.

I love you.

More later,
Mom

FEBRUARY 19, 2014

THINKING OF YOU

James, a servant of God and of the Lord Jesus Christ,
to the twelve tribes which are scattered abroad, greeting.
My brethren, count it all joy when ye fall into divers temptations;
Knowing this, that the trying of your faith worketh patience.
James 1:1–3 (KJV)

My Son,

How are you?

This is not a true letter from me. Somehow, I misplaced the letter for this day. Either I have thrown it away or discarded it with the thing I gave to the Salvation Army yesterday. So, I am just sending you this note to try to keep my promise to you. It is now very hard for me with Mom. I don't seem to have a moment of my own. But I am very excited about downsizing and prioritizing.

Like you—this is a life-changing experience, and many things are no longer very important.

More next time,
Mom, with love

THINKING OF YOU

My Dear Son,

Don't forget to pray. How are you?

You are what you eat, remember?

I have enclosed a letter Little Jackie wrote you some time ago and asked me to mail. I just found it.

Several people have asked for your new address. Should I give it to them?

Mrs. Carmelita Rivera Cullens said you have been kind to her family. She is one of the people who wants to write you.

Eddie Bow has not been well. Rev Meeks's daughter is getting married. Allene said you sent her a very moving letter.

I am very busy today, will write more.

Mom

P.S. Jackie is in Finland for 3 months.

A Psalm of David

The Lord is my light and my salvation; whom shall I fear? the Lord is the strength of my life; of whom shall I be afraid?

When the wicked, even mine enemies and my foes, came upon me to eat up my flesh, they stumbled and fell.

Though an host should encamp against me, my heart shall not fear: though war should rise against me, in this will I be confident.

One thing have I desired of the Lord, that will I seek after; that I may dwell in the house of the Lord all the days of my life, to behold the beauty of the Lord, and to enquire in his temple.

For in the time of trouble he shall hide me in his pavilion: in the secret of his tabernacle shall he hide me; he shall set me up upon a rock.

And now shall mine head be lifted up above mine enemies round about me: therefore will I offer in his tabernacle sacrifices of joy; I will sing, yea, I will sing praises unto the Lord.

Hear, O Lord, when I cry with my voice: have mercy also upon me, and answer me.

When thou saidst, Seek ye my face; my heart said unto thee, Thy face, Lord, will I seek.

Hide not thy face far from me; put not thy servant away in anger: thou hast been my help; leave me not, neither forsake me, O God of my salvation.

When my father and my mother forsake me, then the Lord will take me up.

Teach me thy way, O Lord, and lead me in a plain path, because of mine enemies.

Deliver me not over unto the will of mine enemies: for false witnesses are risen up against me, and such as breathe out cruelty.

I had fainted, unless I had believed to see the goodness of the Lord in the land of the living.

Wait on the Lord: be of good courage, and he shall strengthen thine heart: wait, I say, on the Lord.

Psalms 27 (KJV)

THINKING OF YOU

My Son,

God is good!

Whenever I receive a letter from you, my heart leaps.

I haven't written because I haven't had an address for you. My mail arrived from Washington earlier this week from Mr. Corry, and I am not opening it this morning. I will not read your letters until later this evening when my life is quiet.

I encourage you to pray without ceasing, remain in service to God, and help someone each and every day. I am so excited to hear from you. I will write you again tonight. My mother is very difficult for me now. The stroke has not left her the same, and she requires a lot of my time.

Today, the men are here to begin the work on my house, so I will stay home and make oxtail stew for Allene and Sandy.

I love you more each day. I hope you are eating well. Jesse, you are what you eat. You are not junk.

Read your Bible.

While on the college tour with 78 young city students, I went to church Palm Sunday. About 30 of the young people on the tour joined the church. It was a church in Alabama. I thought it a great sign.

I received a blessing about restorative justice, and determined that the process is a little more difficult than thought.

Forgiveness is not a concept that is guided by personal benefit nor is nonviolence. Restorative justice and nonviolence are exemplified best during the crucifixion and resurrection.

1. The soldier's ear that Peter cut off (Jesus put it back on)
2. Peter's disowning Jesus
3. Judas. Had Jesus called Judas out at dinner, he may not have been crucified
4. Doubting Thomas

I believe Jesus' ultimate act of nonviolence was his response to Judas. Think about this. Perhaps we can talk on Mother's Day?

Love you,
Mom

THINKING OF YOU

My Dear Son,

Don't forget to pray.

I can't wait to discuss the Crucifixion and the Resurrection with you.

I feel this event in history is perhaps the most documented account of restorative justice and nonviolent conflict resolution.

Please read it so we can discuss this event when we are together.

Got to go.

With every beat of my heart I love you,
Mom

LOVING YOU

Thou shalt love your neighbor as thyself.
Matthew 19:19 (KJV)

My Son,

Hope you are well!

Just a short note. Wednesday Grandma Helen fell in the wash-room. Rev is down in SC with her now; Yusef is there with him. We are trying to find a family member to go down and stay with her. She is in the hospital now.

I am just getting help with my living room ceiling, which has been a nightmare. The workers trickle in occasionally. But I am grateful. Yusef sent me a picture of Momma Helen. She doesn't look like the grandma we knew, it makes me sad.

I miss and love you very much,
Mama

THINKING OF YOU

Dear Son,

Don't forget to pray.

How are you? I must apologize for not writing sooner, but I have been in over my head with the convention. I feel some of the people on the team, sometimes unconsciously, defeat all we are trying to do. All motion ain't progress.

Just because I have not written to you does not mean you are not always in my prayers and thoughts.

I pray that God guides your every step and strengthens your body, mind, and soul.

I hope your family is doing well.

I meet people every day, and they always, always ask about you and wish you well.

I hope you are still reading your Bible?

Oh, by the way, Rev Otis told me of his visit with you. His visit was a real surprise to me, as a matter of fact, shocking—especially with Joe joining him. Well, I don't know what to make of the visit. I hope the visit lifted your spirits.

Judy said she is going to visit you also.

I saw Jerri Wright at the convention. She said, once again, her date has been changed to October. Everyone wishes her the best. But I worry about her optimism; it must be terrible to be so uncertain about your future.

Please let me hear from you. I am returning to Washington on Monday.

Don Harris goes faithfully by your house to take care of your lawn and check on the house. He asked me to tell you that.

I love you all the time,

Mom

P.S. By the way, her dad sent your dad a lovely letter.

June 6, 2014

LOVE YOU

Be content whatever your state.—Paul[1]

My Son,

Hi. Are you okay? I have not heard a word as to your welfare. Are you eating better? Did you get your books and things from Butner? I heard from someone who knew you at Butner. They write often . . . encouraging letters often.

Well, Rev Barrow is not well. Rev Morris is in charge of her affairs, and there are lots of complaints against him regarding Rev B's condition. People don't understand, it is very, very difficult to take care of someone who is dying. Sister Claudette went to see her and raised a stink about her condition. I have tried to maintain a healthy distance in this matter because it may get very messy. By the way, Sis Claudette sends you the *Final Call*; she asked me do you receive them?

Though invited, Rev Sharpton didn't come to the convention. All of the people were there, from Rev Al Sampson to Dwight. I saw his full Chicago team, that's good information. Maureen didn't come—rumor has it she's very angry because he appointed Rev Livingston State Head of his organization and placed him over her. Mind you, Livingston left a fine (so I am told) church for this new job with Rev Al.

We are busy assessing our manpower; we will have to cut our staff severely. This makes me very unhappy.

It has rained damn near every day this summer. We are having a tough time.

For the first time in years, the Business luncheon outsold the Women's luncheon. I saw Earl Graves's sons there. This was a big surprise. One of the Black advertisement companies commented on the panel that, in several years, we have suffered a loss of 75% of the Black business during this period.

There is a lot of pain in our society. Never before have I experienced this feeling of sadness. I am praying more and more these days. It seems as if we have all gone too far and now we are at the cliff. We are having uncivilized experiences of revolutionary proportions. The street murders, drive-by shootings, children killing children, parents killing their children and vice versa. Jesse, for the first time, I saw the Gay Pride parade . . . my, my, my. This parade, I feel, is not good for their cause.

I will have to let go and let God. You do the same.

I love you,
Mom

LOVING YOU ALWAYS

My Son,

Don't forget to pray.

How are you? I hope you are eating fruits and vegetables because you are what you eat.

Well, Alderman Beavers came home a week ago.

He came to 50th on the Lake. Everyone has been having welcome home parties for him.

He wants to do something about the prison system. Someone made him a wallet with "The Hog with the Big Nuts" printed on it. People were very happy for his return. So am I. He introduced me to his daughter; she is quite pleasant.

Things are very slow around here. We have so much construction going on; you won't recognize Hyde Park or downtown.

Oh, someone is building a first-class tennis court in, of all places, Englewood. Can you believe that? The city is putting in a new pipe under our street in my neighborhood and in Hyde Park. Hyde Park will have 23 eateries. I expect 71st will be next. Anderson Thomas's wife just sold her house.

The couple across the street from me, I've forgotten their names, sold their house and moved. My neighbors, the doctors who live in the Ramsey Lewis house, said they may be moving in a year or so.

I will return to Washington next week after Leah graduates. That's all for now.

Let go and let God guide you,
Mom

JUNE 11, 2014

THINKING OF YOU

My Son,

Don't forget to pray.

I hope you are eating well. I love and miss you all the time.

Leah just graduated. She is on her way to W. Young High. She is very excited because that's where her dad went. Skye is sad because she is being left behind at school. However, Yusef may be transferring her to another school. Noah is about 5'9". I don't know how or when that happened.

I had lunch with Jessye Norman. She is on a book tour. She is a very fascinating woman, and I enjoyed her very much.

Jackie is back from Finland, Germany. She had a wonderful time. Jesse,

I think about you every day, and I worry too.

I received a warm letter from a man in NY who spoke highly of you. I will save the letter for your return. You will find it most uplifting.

I love you,
Mom

LOVING YOU EVERY MINUTE

My Son,

How are you? This you must know, I love you from head to toe.

Did you receive your things from NC? Your books? If not, I will send them to you again. People today are meaner than I have ever known them to be. People are very worried that you are not treated well. But you should not worry about the indifference you will endure here; there is an all-seeing God. You must always rise above all foolishness, as you have been taught; and be of good cheer, so that God will protect.

Let no one have power over you but God. Remain strong in the faith. Let go and let God. Do it for you.

As I am writing to you this very moment, Munir Muhammad is tonight saying very kind things about you. This is a very pleasant surprise for me. It's moments like this that lets me know God is listening. We are pulling for you, Jesse.

It's left up to you.

I pay for your storage each month. People want your address. You have no idea how many people want to write to you.

I have tried to explain to people you are only allowed a few stamps. They are surprised that one who is confined would be denied as many stamps as he or she can afford.

Will write more next time. I love you and miss you,

Mom

Kisses

June 16, 2014

LOVING YOU

My Son,

Don't forget to pray, and you are what you eat.

How are you?

I am still preparing the house and PUSH. Yusef has agreed to help manage some of the things at PUSH. Lord knows we need the help. Alanna is very helpful.

Oh, I almost forgot: one of the men who was released from jail because of his innocence, after having served 30 years, is now in Cook County. The staff found him on the Internet. It seems as though he may return to prison. It is very sad. He received a lot of money, and it has created a lot of trouble for him.

I hope you are reading and eating properly. This is very important. I worry about your health, Jesse. I hope you are okay.

Well, the world keeps on turning. I am tired tonight. Will write more tomorrow.

Love you.

Mom

THINKING OF YOU

I love you and miss you very much.

How are you? Please don't forget to pray.

It's convention time, and everything is up in the air, as it is every year. Somehow, we prevail.

I hope you are well. People always, always ask about you, and wish you well. You will see.

Mom

LOVING YOU ALWAYS

For God so loved the world, that he gave his only begotten
Son, that whosoever believeth in him should not perish,
but have everlasting life.
John 3:16 (KJV)

My Son,

I thought I could visit you this week, but I could not get away. May I come this coming weekend?

How are you? I want to inform you about this past week. Almost nothing was done to get out the vote for the Dems this election.

I couldn't believe what I saw. Will tell you more when we get together. Don't let anyone break your spirit, and stay focused.

Now, are you eating better? How is your back? Did you let the people in charge know you have a history of foot problems and back issues? Are they aware of your health history? I worry about you all the time.

Last night, I went to the announcement of the Library of Congress as the permanent repository for the HistoryMakers Collection. I was, along with the HistoryMakers founder, deeply moved when I shared with Julieanna our first meeting in the doctor's office. She was at the office to address her broken foot, and I was there because I had been in the train wreck from Washington to Chicago.

She was deeply moved because I remembered the enthusiasm she had for this idea. Now this idea is a great success. I am very happy for

her. All the VIPs were there: Holder, Jordan, Jarrett, etc.
Will tell you more.

Got to go,
Mom

July 6, 2014

THINKING OF YOU

My Son,

Sorry I sent you a letter with the wrong date. I was very tired.

My letter to Muhammad was returned today. I may have misspelled his name. I have written him again to see.

In my Smart Car yesterday, I found a reminder of you. You left your gym shoes in the back of the Smart Car. I am going to leave them in the car until you return.

I am worried about some of your visitors, only because they have never held an interest in you. Why now? Can they be interested in your health? If so, why? Who are they discussing you with, and what for? There is so much deceit surrounding you. Please be careful.

Read and stay prayerful.

Love you,
Mom

THINKING OF YOU

My Son,

How are you? I hope all is well.

Today was a very good day. We had a family meeting this morning to discuss the convention and a plan for the reorganization of PUSH. We began with prayer. We thanked God for you, and we all prayed for your safety.

The PUSH board has been reorganized: we have new board members and are hiring a building manager, etc.

I think we will have a major cut in our staff. We are having a difficult time, but so are many organizations at this time.

Thank Heavens we are much closer because of you. If not but for one reason: We worry about you together.

Remember . . . united we stand, divided we fall. I saw this with Malcolm X's children while at the hospital with their mom, the King children, Ralph's children, and most of all Elijah Muhammad's family. When Elijah died, Wallace decided to change, completely, the organization. In doing so, he dismantled it. And people (the members) became very angry with him for doing so.

He cracked the door, and his enemies came in and devoured him and his new ideas.

Jesse, we are not the reason you are here! As a matter of fact, we've always tried to save you from others and yourself.

This time, you were too far away. This was your choice.

Well good news: I bought you some fishing lures from a house sale. I hope you remember Dr. Hurst, president of Malcolm X

College. The people who live there now are moving and they have as much stuff as I have.

I'll save the lures, about 100 of them, until your return.

Perhaps we can fry the fish you catch with them and add some grits and cheese for breakfast.

I miss you so much. I love you all the time.

I think I told you the South Side is beginning to look like the North Side.

Did I tell you the Lab School is now on Stony Island Ave., where Doctor's Hospital once was? The mayor announced some new and trendy food stores and restaurants will be coming to East 87th St.

More next time. Don't forget to pray.

I love you,
Mom

LOVING YOU

Without a vision, a people perish.
Proverbs 29:18 (KJV)

Dear Son,

I hope you are taking care.

Don't forget to do unto others as you would have them do unto you.

I was very happy to hear from you this evening, if only for a brief moment. Sorry about my cell phone disconnecting our conversation. It does that all the time.

I am glad you had visitors this weekend. Your dad was excited about coming to see you . . . he worries about your well-being.

Rita has been appointed a judge by the governor. She will be sworn in sometime in the week ahead, but she has to be elected in the November election. She will be on the Republican ticket. I am told by her mother she has a great chance of winning. I know she will do well.

Yusef and I are working together to restore the PUSH building. I am excited. It's a lot of work.

I grow vegetables during the summer, so I can put them away for the winter. I have not had a good crop this year. The weather has not helped. Maybe next year.

I have, today, returned some of my furniture to the living room, and we can sit in the room comfortably. I'll keep working, and perhaps it will be completed by your return.

I love and miss you,
Mom

UNDATED #8

My Son,

Each time I hear your voice, my heart leaps. Thank you for calling me.

I love you so much—it's something about the original sin in the Bible and the curse placed on women. The older I grow the clearer my understanding becomes of the curse. The pain endured at birth, the responsibility for nurturing, the amount of self-denial—or denial of self—this is necessary for child rearing. Yet we do it over, and over, and over again because of the joy loving children brings.

The curse—our love—is without conditions . . . and we never stop loving and loving our children. Even at death's door, we are more worried about their welfare than our meeting with the Creator. I understand the responsibility God has visited upon women; and to be a woman makes me very proud.

Are you eating well? I worry for your safety, as do many people.

I told your father you've called me, and I also told him he must have told you to do so. He glowed. That made me happy.

OH, Mr. Corry was in a terrible accident, 5 cars were involved. He, I think, caused the accident. He was the last driver and he rear-ended the driver in front of him. His car was totaled; he is alive. God is Great again.

I am going to Virginia tomorrow to pick up Gertie. Will write you again.

Love you all the time,
Mom

LOVING YOU

My Son,

Don't forget to pray.

How are you? I was very disturbed to hear you were called about your storage. You are aware I have been paying your bill.

I have also been advised that someone close to you is trying to gain access to your storage. I am telling you this so you will know. I don't want to be involved in any foolishness. You can call Mr. Hughes and tell him no one is to have access.

Or send the letter to PUSH, and Alanna can get it to him.

LOVING YOU

My Son,

Don't forget to pray.

Thank you for loving me. God is good to me. My mother is stronger, as will you become. I think of you every day; and when I am not thinking of you, someone will appear and ask about your well-being.

I am very sorry I have not been able to write you every day in the evening. I am so tired, and my days are so very full.

Now you should not need to hear from me so frequently; you should be growing stronger in Christ.

Don has your place very well kept. He is faithful.

OH, did I tell you, Ray has a baby now? He babysits during the day. He told me he fell asleep while holding the baby and dropped it. The baby didn't get hurt, thanks be to God.

Susana Cepeda is not well and is living in China with her son. Maurice is not well. But God has given all of us another day.

I love you very much. Remember Mandela, Dr. King, Gandhi, Harold Washington, and a host of others made this stop on life's journey. It is a bump in the road.

You will be better for this. Life and your time will be important, and many things will have less importance.

I love you so very much,
Mom

THINKING OF YOU

Dear Son,

God is Great!

How are you? Are you eating better? Don't forget to pray. I just wanted to drop you a quick line, just to let you know I am thinking of you.

Can't wait to talk with you about all the things that are happening. It's really a big mess.

This morning, I am driving Mom back to Virginia. She thinks it's around the corner. I must leave early because I don't see so well at night.

She doesn't like Mr. Corry sometimes because she is jealous of him helping me to help her. Isn't that crazy?

What about the militarized police in the USA? That has lots of people concerned.

The stroke has left Mom somewhat confused at times.

Jackie wants to visit you next weekend. You should let her know something. I can't wait for your return. I know you will have a lot to talk about.

I love you always,
Mom

August 28, 2014

THINKING OF YOU

My Son,

How are you? I hope you remember that you are what you eat.

I have been so happy about your visitors. Corrine said she spoke with you for about 2 hours. She was very glad you looked well. Joe Bee called to tell me she wants to visit you. Even my sister thinks you to be living in some sort of hotel. When I told them you were behind bars, they got mad all over again. They both said, with all these bad people walking around here free, stealing, murdering, and raping women, these people have some nerve.

I went to Macy's today. A Spanish employee came to me to tell me of her father's imprisonment. I saw D. Kyles; he's still fighting, for 11 years, and still may have to go to prison. As you know, Jerri Wright keeps getting her court date changed. It's very crazy out here.

Jackie is very pleased with herself. You've made her very happy. Thank you for loving your sister. She depends on you and looks up to you.

P.S. I slipped and fell the other day . . . much better now. Also, Jan's mother died last night. I love you.

AUGUST 29, 2014

THINKING OF YOU

My Son,

Don't forget to pray.

How are you? I just hung up the phone after speaking to Mrs. Rita Samuels and J. T. Johnson of Atlanta. They want to come to visit you. They, along with several others, have constantly called. I grow so tired of trying to explain the process to them. I think they think we're special and there is special consideration for us. They just don't know how ordinary we really are. I am always flattered by their thinking.

They really think we don't stand in lines, and I'll never tell. Jesse, talking to my sister Connie just this week, she even thought you are in a special place somewhere. She had no idea you are incarcerated. I couldn't believe her, as close as she is to my business, that she had no idea you are not in a hotel.

Many rumors regarding Ferguson: The young people believe the police that shot the boy was on drugs and the police didn't arrest the policeman because they would have had to test his blood?

What about that? There is little faith in the justice system. That makes me very sad.

Jan's mother's funeral is Friday. We will handle the repast.

Yusef and I have been spending time with your father, trying to encourage him to restructure the organization.

Little Jonathan spent the summer at Carnegie Mellon in a math program . . . He loved it.

Skye passed the test for the Lab School, and she is happy also.
I am in the dentist office again.

> Love you more,
> Mom

LOVING YOU ALWAYS

My Son,

Don't forget to pray.

I love you, first of all. Yesterday, I had a day I should at least try to explain or describe. Normally, while working in the house, my companion is NPR or TV. Today, it is TV. Even if I am not watching TV, it is on. I surf occasionally, never mindful of where I stop the remote. Then, I go about completing whatever I was doing before.

While in the kitchen, I heard a preacher discussing 2 Corinthians 4:8–10. He wore glasses, a royal blue suit, and I believe, a pink tie.

I stopped for a few minutes only to discover that he was almost to the end of his sermon. He appeared to be interesting, but he was closing and inviting his viewers to join him again.

So, I went on with my day.

I arrived at PUSH at about 9:00 or 10:00, met with Rev Wilson and several others until about 1:30. Then I thought, before I left, I would peek in and say "hello" to Rev.

When I opened Rev's door, this preacher whom I had just seen on TV was visiting Rev. I said to him, "Didn't I just see you on TV?" He said, "Maybe, I am on all the time." I said, "This morning you spoke from Corinthians." I described his outfit to him because I wasn't sure this was the same person. He told me his name . . . I don't remember it even now. He is a bishop and a friend of yours. He said you have spent a considerable amount of time with him and he has supported you. He said you have visited his home. I guess he lives out there where Bishop Trotter lives. He said he was in court with us and he has met me several times before.

I would be willing to swear on a stack of Bibles I have never seen him in my life.

Tell me the chances of me randomly changing channels and stopping to hear an inspirational message from a stranger, then stopping by the office and seeing the same someone in the office whom I just saw on TV—and discovering he is friend of my son.

God is in all things. All things.

I love you,
Mom

I LOVE YOU

My Son,

Don't forget to pray.

Did you ever get your things from Butner? The weather has been unusual. I wish I could surprise you and paint your house for you, but that would mean you will have less to do when you return. Everyone is expecting you to return in November. And when I tell them you won't be home, they argue me down because someone has said that is when you are returning.

I, along with many others, thank you sincerely for your great work, Jesse. You did a great work, and many are grateful. And I am not going to let anyone take your credit from you.

Remember Nixon: even though he resigned in shame, he is still Mr. President and has an honorable place in history. So will you.

I am not ashamed of you, Jesse. You must mature.

She. Had. It. To. happens. We are going to move on. We have more work to do.

We are headed towards moral collapse, and we all know what happens after that. Einstein, after splitting the atom: "As of this day, everything has changed but man's thinking." Therefore, we are headed for unparalleled destruction.

Jesus tried to change the heart of man, but failed. He said, "Greater things shall we do, if we believe." I believe the heart of man can be changed; but it is some very difficult work, and we must not give up.

You mean the world to me,

Mom

LOVE YOU SO MUCH

My Son,

Don't forget to pray.

I love you very much. We are getting ready for more war. I guess we haven't learned anything yet.

Thank God, today was uneventful. Rev is in California tonight. He is taking a late plane back to Chicago tonight. All the old folks are doing fine. Thanks be to God.

I hope you are still reading. I am going to send you some books next week. You must continue to read.

Sandy and I would like to visit you soon. Can you let me know when we can visit?

Jesse, do you feel safe? How are they treating you? Many are worried for you. With all this mistreatment of Blacks, people are very worried about you. And so am I, Jesse. Your diet is very important . . . and your medicine. Please take care of yourself. I Love You.

Mom

LOVING YOU

My Son,

Don't forget to pray.

You are on my mind. It is very cold today. This is what I love about Chicago: unpredictability. I may have told you before: Rita has been appointed a judge in Ohio. She is Republican, and I think she will win. We'll know in November. I am going to send her a contribution.

Yusef and Sandy are reading, they say, a very interesting book on Joe Kennedy titled, *The Patriot*. I'll send it to you. I am going to read it myself. I hope you will watch Ken Burns's *The Roosevelts* on Sunday. This documentary took Ken Burns 6 yrs to produce. I can't wait to see it. It is a big thing, according to the media.

Oh, I will also send you *Mayor for Life*, Marion Barry. On my next train ride, I will begin his book.

I think of you all the time. Stay well.

I love you,
Mom

September 15, 2014

I LOVE YOU

For God so loved the world, that he gave his only begotten Son, that whosoever believeth in him should not perish, but have everlasting life.
John 3:16 (KJV)

My Son,

Don't forget to pray.

I just finished watching Ken Burns's *The Roosevelts*—great documentary. It's about 10:27, I'm surfing stations . . . and there he is. This time, I have his name: Bishop Simon Gordon. His message is from Ecclesiastes 3:9–14, titled "It's Irreversible." He is also promoting all of his government programs.

I have now bumped into him, within a few days, 3 times. Well, let me see what this means.

Jesse, everything is in divine order. It's all good.

Love you too much,

Mom

P.S. Everyone thinks you are coming home soon?

LOVING YOU ALWAYS

Dear Son,

How are you? This stationery? A little info or history about it:

The design, "The Bird," was created by Ms. Barbara Proctor's firm in 1971 as an identifiable symbol that people could associate with me. I have been cleaning house since you have been away. I found this stationery that I used as an invitation to invite women to the PUSH Expo International Women's Luncheons.

My son, that was in 1971—a lifetime ago. And yet, for me, just yesterday.

I think of you back then, as a little boy, and I love you even more now than I did then. I am very proud of your efforts and all of your work.

I always try to address you as Congressman Jackson because your title represents your work, and everyone hits a bump in the road at some point. They may stumble and may fall down. But the good that is done remains.

Nixon resigned, and he is still Mr. President. Marion Barry will always be Mayor. Clinton was impeached; he is still Mr. President. Just call the roll.

They even call Bush Mr. President.

Pity is poison.

Keep your head up. Let no one have power over you but Christ. Continue to encourage and inspire others.

You are a good person, and many, many people are aware of this.

Try to eat well. Love everybody. Most of all, don't forget to pray. God is not finished with you.

> Keep the Faith. Let No One Break Your Spirit,
> Mom

THINKING OF YOU

My Son,

Don't forget to pray, always.

How are you? I won't write much today or this night because I just finished paying my bills and I have been out all day. Allene asked me to tell you "hello" for her. I am going to give Dara your address as soon as I complete this letter.

Your dad was very happy to see you Wednesday. He loves you so much, but that's nothing much because you've got a lot of love all around you.

You won't recognize Hyde Park. I don't know where they have found all this money, but they did.

It's 11:00 p.m. I want to wash a few things before I go to bed.

Will write more tomorrow.

I will love you always,
Mom

OCTOBER 24, 2014

LOVING YOU ALWAYS

My Son,

Don't forget to pray.

Boy, did I have fun seeing and talking with you. It made my heart feel so good, being with you.

I had intended to write you immediately upon my return, but I came down with a cold and I haven't felt well.

As a Blk, you know I can't go out of the house with a cold—you know why. You should see people clearing the way for me. So I will remain inside until it clears.

Jesse, you must eat better because you are what you eat. Take good care of yourself, and please be open for discussions.

I will write you more the next time.

Your Mom . . . Who Loves You Very Much

I LOVE YOU

My Son,

Paul said, "I have learned to be content in whatever state I am in."[1]

I am going to try to see you soon. I wish I could do this for you, but I can't.

I know how good you are. Don't let anyone make you doubt your goodness.

God is on our side . . . just you wait and see the goodness of God. Thank you for reviving my faith.

You know it is always tested.

God is Great,
Mom

NOVEMBER 25, 2014

THINKING OF YOU

My Son,

Don't forget to pray.

How are you? Several times, I have stopped to take the time to write, but there are so many interruptions. So, I have stacks of unfinished letters to you, filed in a drawer. I'll give them to you when you return.

This letter, I am writing while on the train to Chicago for Thanksgiving. I can only write when we stop rocking and reeling. I am also reading a great book—two, as a matter of fact. One is Steve Biko, *I Write What I Like*, and I am rereading Alive Toffler's *Future Shock*. A must read for you is Steve Biko's description of Blackness. Wonderful.

Well this morning my phone began ringing at 5:30. I refused to answer it because I knew something was wrong or it was bad news. Now I let bad news wait until I have time for it. Finally, I decided to return the calls at about 6:00 or 6:30, and that's when I heard my hero, Marion Barry, had become a part of the ages. When I last saw him, he was not well . . . or he didn't look well.

I loved and admired him so much. I think he is the greatest politician of our time. In my book, it takes a lot of a political person to upstage Adam Clayton Powell and Daley, but Marion has absolutely beat them all. Also, he and your dad created the Black middle class that has been witnessed from the '70s through the '90s.

The John Johnsons, the George Johnsons, the Gardners, and so many others . . . an era that has, sadly ended. And the evidence is apparent.

Now about Bill. This sounds like Bill Cosby wanted to change his agency or something, and someone decided to kick his butt. The movie *Valley of the Dolls* was a hit back then; people need to review it. Pills were the rage back then, and many, many wannabe stars were taking them. Question: After being tricked into taking one pill, who returns to be tricked again and again? You wanted some more? All these virtuous women . . . didn't they know he was married—each one fooled, yet in another woman's home? Women can't have it both ways. And, did they all get the same memo, at the same time, to show up for this great confession on the same day? I love Bill and Camille Cosby for all the good they have done for many, including me. And I am sick and tired of people attempting to instruct on which Blk person we should like.

What about Lewinsky? She said, "My mistake was falling in love with my boss." Question: What were the job qualifications for her at 21 (to work anywhere near the President)? Who recommended her? Could she be replaced? Most of all, did she know the President had a wife, or did it matter? These girls should be more responsible and trustworthy. They all need Jesus.

When I see you, we have much to talk about.

With every beat of my heart I love you,
Mom

P.S. You see how foolish women can make a mess of things.

December 1, 2014

LOVING YOU

My Son,

I love you. Don't forget to pray. God had to give you a burden so that you will lean on him. My faith is strong.

I am returning to Washington tomorrow for Mayor Barry. Thank God for all he has done for our country and our people. Please take care of yourself so God can use you also.

Will write more next time.

I love you with all my heart,
Mom

I LOVE YOU ALWAYS

My Son,

Don't forget to pray.

I love you. Things are moving so rapidly all around us. Yesterday, we buried Marion Barry. Berna called tonight to tell me Walter Washington's wife, Mary, was in the *Washington Post* because she, too, has died. Tomorrow, I will see if I have another funeral to attend.

I miss you so much, and I think of you all the time. I don't have the time I once had, even to write you. Owe the Feds more than ever in income tax, yet I have less. I guess this is the Joe Lewis and Ali story? But the people are close to understanding, and I don't feel bad about any of this (Smile).

What about New York's Eric Garner? Even on video we didn't see what we saw? With Michael Brown, we don't, or shouldn't, believe all the witnesses? "Hands Up": the establishment, has credibility problems. I will come to see you, so you will know what is going on.

I hope you are still reading? Don't worry about anything. All is well. Mom and Grandma Helen are waiting for you, as are so many others.

Most of all, people want to see you. They don't trust where you are. I try to assure people you are okay. But they must see for themselves.

These are very strange times, but good for the country.

Stay strong. Love God with all your heart.
Can't wait to see you.

With my heart I love you,
Mom

December 8, 2014

LOVING YOU EACH DAY

Trust in the Lord with all thine heart; and lean not unto thine own
understanding. In all thy ways acknowledge him, and he shall direct thy paths.
Proverbs 3:5–6 (KJV)

My Son,

You are what you eat. How are you?

This year has almost passed, and a wonderful year is about to begin again. And I am so very grateful to God. I have my family, and most of my friends have made it. Thanks be to God. Oftentimes, we are never grateful until we look back and think about what could have happened.

Now, I thank God all the time for small things that I, during my youth, took for granted.

Who would have thought we all would be at this point at this time? I know I wouldn't have. Yet I am a much better person because of my life's happenstances. Every time I thought I couldn't, I did it better. And everything I didn't get or do, I don't miss.

I am enjoying life at this time, my son. I hope you are using this time wisely? Read, read, and listen to everything around you. When you return home, all of the sounds will be very important. The view from your window, the birds flying overhead, the freedom the insects have in the prison . . . everything about where you have been will become very important to you.

I miss and love you very much.

Will discuss these current events when I see you. There is so

[195]

much disappointment and sadness in society. However, all is well, and this too shall pass.

My love always,
Mom

LOVING YOU ALWAYS

My Son,

Prayer works.

How are you? I am on the train returning to Chicago for the Christmas holidays. At Costco, I purchased this wonderful book I am now reading: *Miracles* by Eric Metaxas, a *New York Times* bestselling author of *Bonhoeffer: Pastor, Martyr, Prophet, Spy*.

Miracles . . . what they are, why they happen, and how they can change your life. I am very impressed.

One of the questions raised by this author: If we thank God for the good things, why not thank Him for the bad? And I quote:

The author of the *Gulag Archipelago*, Aleksandr Solzhenitsyn, who suffered for twenty years in the hellish prison camps he describes in that book, wrote, "Bless you prison, bless you for being in my life. For there, lying upon the rotting prison straw, I came to realize that the object of life is not prosperity, as we are made to believe, but the maturity of the human soul."

This does not mean that Newton would have chosen to go through his trials or that Solzhenitsyn in any way enjoyed the terrible suffering of his imprisonment. But it means that in retrospect they can see that God used difficulties to bless them in the long run.

Of course, no one wants to suffer. Let's be clear about that. Let's also be clear that that is normal and healthy. It is understanding that as much as we wish to avoid suffering, there is more to life than merely avoiding suffering. In fact, good can come out of suffering. If we know this, it changes how we suffer. It gives it meaning. So what we desperately do want to avoid is not merely suffering, but suffering without meaning.

If our suffering has a purpose, it is infinitely easier to bear than if our suffering has no purpose and no larger meaning. When a mother endures childbirth, she knows that it is leading to something life changing and glorious.

Viktor Frankl, who endured the death camps of the Third Reich wrote in his book *Man's Search for Meaning,* "In some ways, suffering ceases to be suffering at the moment it finds a meaning. He also wrote that "those who have a why to live, can bear with almost any how." [1]

I have written several paragraphs from this book; as soon as I arrive, I am going to send you several copies so you can share this reading with your friends.

A little joke I just heard. No, I'll tell you when I see you. It's about some bird flying south.

I love you so much,
Mom

I THANK GOD FOR YOU

My Son,

Don't forget to pray.

I love you so much. I will not dance this Christmas, nor will I have libations.

I will pray for all who are denied access to their families on this Holy day.

I was awake most of the night with my new read, *Miracles* by Eric Metaxas. The book is about 340 pages. The first half of this book is very weighted. However, the second half has left me a little disappointed. I will send it to you. Please read it. I want your opinion. At least finish the first part of the book.

On the train, I was seated in the Old Folk section: the lower coach. Two women sat near me coughing all night. One woman was coughing so badly, she couldn't lie down. She sat up all night. She was very ill, and that made me very sad.

Never did I think I would be one of the old people. That's who was in my section.

Now I realize how important it is to protect one's health, or we will live to regret our abuse of this gift of health.

Do take care of yourself. If not for yourself, for those who love you.

I love you so much,
Mom

THINKING OF YOU ALWAYS

My Son,

Don't forget to pray.

How are you? How was Christmas? We surely missed you, and all asked about you. I have, around here somewhere, two letters I have written to you that I can't seem to find. I'll just save them for your return.

Don Harris said your family came into town Saturday or Sunday of last week. Rev said he has not heard from them, and Sandi has not returned his many calls. Yusef said he saw them Wednesday night, I think. I don't know what is going on, but your father is upset and sad. He is tired of calling and not having his calls returned. I don't know what is going on.

This year, we have had so many invitations to events for the holidays. I have attended many of them, solely for all the neighborhood gossip. Things are not so good. Someone or some people are stealing the Christmas decorations from our neighbors' yards, and the neighbors are mad as hell with Leslie. By the way, I love her. Tom Lewis always spoke highly of her. People are dissatisfied with the mayor, hmmmm . . .

D. Kyles lost his 23-yr-old son, the one with the heart transplant, in a car accident the day before Christmas. Rev Humphrey, Sylvia Branch, and Rev Johnny Coleman all went to glory; and God ain't finished yet.

I didn't clean the chitterlings this year. I'll wait until you come home.

You are All-ways on my mind,

Mom

December 27, 2014

LOVING YOU

My Son,

Don't forget to pray!

How are you today? Yesterday evening after I had written to you, I spoke with little Jesse III. His spirit was so high. He was on his way to see the wrestling game. Rev was equally excited. He said all the children had a very nice time. I didn't get to see them to say "hello," but maybe sometime today or tomorrow I will get with Jesse. I don't know if Jessica is here?

There have been many TV interviews about the Congressional Frat House because someone new has purchased it. I don't know, did you ever live there? Of course, Durbin has been all over the tube. They've made it sound like a dorm.

As you can see, I am beginning to have problems writing. Something is going wrong with my thumb. Doing things that require its use is painful. I am going to check on this when I go back to the doctor. Growing old is an ass kicker. I didn't know I would become one of the old people.

I thank God I am still growing. I have learned as of recent in order to grow, I must let go . . . growing fast.

Got to go to be with Sylvia for her homegoing.

Love you always,
Mom

THINKING OF YOU

Blessed are the peacemakers.
Matthew 5:9 (KJV)

My Son,

The year is gone. Over. Thank God!

Now we can begin again.

My mother said, "The older one grows, the quicker the year goes."

The office was open 1/2 day today.

Most of my time was spent with Bettye, Mag, and Rev Wilson. After the office, Rev Wilson and I had a light lunch at Rosebud on Taylor St. I forgot how great this restaurant is. I haven't been there in, I'm sure, 25 years. The Rosebud on Taylor has an old-world elegance. I can't wait for your return so we can have dinner there. I ordered a salad with my meal, and the salad had cucumbers and really green leafy lettuce in it. Wonderful evening dining and watching the snow falling.

When we left, the streets were covered with snow. Just another beautiful Chicago winter day. I love this place.

The weatherman said we may have 6 inches of snow tonight, and that's OK with me.

You all laugh at my Smart Car, but I love it. During the snow, everyone says, "Be careful." But when I get stuck in the snow, we get out and almost lift the car out of it. People volunteer to help me with my car.

I took Rev Wilson home. I didn't know her husband had a heart attack last year. He is not very well.

Also, Lester McKeaver's daughter is not well, I think.

I love you so much,
Mom

THINKING OF YOU

My Son,

Don't forget to pray.

Now I have taken a deep breath and tried to make sense of the conversation we had briefly the other day. By the way, this is my third attempt to commit my feelings to paper. I am going to come to see you, and we can discuss our concerns further.

Love,
Mom

January 30, 2015

I LOVE YOU

For God so loved the world, that he gave his only begotten Son, that whosoever believeth in him should not perish, but have everlasting life.
John 3:16 (KJV)

My Son,

I love you so very much. I am very, very proud of you, my son. You have had, unlike many, the challenge of living up to others' expectations. You have done well, and so many are grateful for the many good things you have caused to happen for them.

Even though you are a great thinker and a brilliant speaker, you have expressed a great love for reading and fishing. I love knowing these things about you. Oh yes, and taking care of your lawn and your house . . . Knowing this about you makes my heart beat more calmly.

I don't write you as often now because I feel you to be much stronger in your faith and your reliance on God. God is Great! I hope your visit went well with your dad.

Make sure you get the names so you can stay in touch with the many friends you have made while detained.

Did you receive the books . . . *Miracles* and *Slavery by Another Name?*

I am working on the house in Washington with James McIntosh. He always asks about you. My Christmas wreath has been converted into a St. Patrick's Day/Birthday wreath. I did it in celebration of our day of birth. Also, the Christmas wreath was so large, I don't have any place to put it but back on the door. I think it's really cute. Mr. Corry provided the pictures. He wants your address so he can write you. He has asked me many times. I told him he didn't need to write you because he has been a loyal friend, and I thank God for him. By the way, he even volunteered to drive me each time I have seen you. By the way, he drove your car back to Washington, no advance notice, and your wife never thanked him. He is a true friend.

Oh Angela, Santita's friend, wants to visit you; she could be helpful to you. I need an answer.

As a man thinketh, so is he.[1]

Don't forget the rich experience.

Love you,
Mom

THINKING OF YOU

My Son,

Don't forget to pray.

For Your Future:

"For I know the plans I have for you," declares the Lord, "plans to prosper you and not to harm you, plans to give you hope and a future."—Jeremiah 29:11 (KJV)

"Do not conform any longer to the world, but be transformed by the renewing of your mind. Then you will be able to test and approve what God's will is—his good, pleasing, and perfect will."—Romans 12:2 (KJV)

Hope to see you soon,
Your Mom

P.S. I hope you will be permitted to see the picture.

I LOVE YOU ALL DAY LONG

My Son,

Don't forget to pray.

I am late tonight. Thank you for the card. It is always wonderful to hear from you. I love you so much. I have no words to explain the burden of a mom and her love for her child. Every mother is not a mom, and I am surely a mom five times.

The painter came over to fix my lights tonight. I just bought a radio for you—it's called Sirius. It's wonderful, can't wait for you to hear it.

Can't wait to see you.

Things are different . . . and yet the same. Will explain when I see you.

I love you with all my heart,

Mom

LOVING YOU ALWAYS

Finally, my brethren, be strong in the Lord, and in the power of his might. Put on the whole armour of God, that ye may be able to stand against the wiles of the devil.
Above all, taking the shield of faith, wherewith ye shall be able to quench all the fiery darts of the wicked.
Ephesians 6:10-11, 16(KJV)

My Son,

Don't forget to pray.

How are you? You are what you eat. I do so look forward to your return. So we may live again.

Your family understands, all too well, the impact confinement has on a family. I believe because our government is constantly studying the cause and effect of social conditions on a people, they too are aware of the cruel impact this act has on families (mean-spirited people).

Since you have been away, some things have changed, yet much remains the same. In Washington, most of the poor and middle class are almost totally removed. Where they have been relocated only heaven knows.

In Chicago, of course, you are aware of the closing of 50 schools in the Blk community. Well, the agreement was to close 100 schools; and I promise you, it may take more time to get this done . . . it will be done.

These things are painful to me.

I miss talking to you so much.

My spiritual self is souring. It is during this darkness that we see God.

Stay strong.

God Is Good,
Mom

FEBRUARY 24, 2015

I LOVE YOU

My Son,

Don't forget to pray.

Everything is in Divine Order.

The thought for today:

You gain strength, courage and confidence by every experience in which you really stop to look fear in the face. You are able to say to yourself, "I have lived through this . . . I can take the next thing that comes along" . . . You must do the thing you think you cannot do.—Eleanor Roosevelt[1]

Just finished painting my bathroom. The painter is coming to help me hang some wallpaper, if the paint is dry tomorrow.

It is now midnight. I must get up early in order to be the bird that catches the worm.

Mom coughs all night long. I am sure she is taking something too strong for her.

Yusef's baby came too early; the baby was due in April. I am sure his wife was trying to hold onto her figure, which most of the young women are doing today. My mom said it's only one way, and that's the right way. You must eat for two.

Mr. Corry has diabetes and something that makes him shake all the time. I still ride with him because he insists on driving. When I am with him, I fear for my life. He should not drive. My mom still wants to drive also, even though the doctor said she shouldn't. After her stroke, they didn't revoke her license. She is more headstrong than ever. Whenever I leave the house, my neighbor Dr. Hill told me, she is constantly trying to find the keys in order to drive herself back to Virginia. So, I am going down to the license place and have them revoke her license to drive.

If you tell me when you are coming home, I will have all the food you love piping hot at the gate.

I love you so much, my son.

P.S. Oh, they mentioned you on the TV; they gave you credit for the Pullman National Park legislation.

I hope the story of the Pullman porters is included.

God is good.

> I Love You Always,
> Mom

LOVING YOU ALWAYS

My Son,
Don't forget to pray.

Happy
Birthday!

P.S. I forgot to tell you about my confrontation with Dyson.

Mom

LOVING YOU ALWAYS

Dear Son,

Don't forget to pray.

How are you? I had hoped to see you for Mother's Day, but things didn't go my way. Your forgiveness campaign is being misunderstood out here!

You should wait until you are on the outside, where you can answer and respond to your feedback.

You are being misunderstood!

You are going to be very disappointed.

Now Mama Helen is in the hospital. She doesn't want to eat. That is not good. Today she is much better, but it is touch and go for now.

I pray that both Grandmas hold on while you are away.

Alanna is quite a good little worker. She is so helpful.

Will write more, hope to see you soon.

Mom

I LOVE YOU

My Son,

Don't forget to pray.

I love you.

Challenges come to those who have the character to face them . . . And opposition and adversity give us a chance to rise to new heights:

"Unless there is opposing wind, a kite cannot rise."
—Chinese proverb[1]

"Trials are blessings in disguise."—Oscar Wilde[2]

I couldn't resist sending you these little gifts.

Love you,
Mom

I'LL BE LOVING YOU ALWAYS

My Son,

Don't forget to pray.

How are you? I love you with my heart. I am proud of you. Let there be no doubt in your mind.

Your house needs painting. I passed it several days ago. Don takes care of your house with a sense of pride. I love him.

Jan's mom's funeral was today at Trinity. We had the repast at PUSH. I couldn't attend the funeral because I have leaks at my house, and have had a time getting someone to take care of them. They came today. Jan spoke brilliantly, they say. She described her mother's decline from birth to death: The child watching one who has given her life be transformed from mom, back to childhood, to infancy.

Jan is absolutely the finest in her family and has the very best heart. Rosie, her daughter, is pregnant with twins and she is so beautiful, and they make me very happy. It's been a long day.

I love you,
Mom

PRAYING FOR YOU

My Son,

I love you very much. How are you? I received a letter from Muhammad. He said they all miss you and they wanted to know how you are doing.

Everyone wants to know how you are doing. Their concern sustains me.

At this time, we are trying to reorganize, which is always difficult to do. Some say everyone should, after 10 yrs, reassess their life and drop the things that are not making their lives better (Percy Sutton).

The problem is, many who have eyes can't see.

I've got my hands full. I remain prayerful.

Love you,
Mom

LOVING YOU ALWAYS

My Son,

Don't forget to pray.

I am so worried about you. How are you? Are you eating properly? We are what we eat, you know.

While cleaning, I just uncovered the wooden flowerpot holder you made for me when you were a boy scout. This morning I was watching the TV in the breakfast room and on the floor before me, covered with tape, was the cloth No. 108. This was one of the labels sent to me from LaMans to be sewn inside your or Jonathan's belongings while at LeMans. Do you remember? Whose number was 108?

I don't know why I keep being reminded of you. Maurice said it may be because I am worried about you.

You will be pleased to see the new highway from 79th to 103rd St. I guess it would be South Shore Drive, the street almost in front of your house.

Santita's birthday is next week. I am going to Detroit with her, and I hope to stop and see Jackie on my way to Detroit.

I passed your house; the lawn was well maintained. Don is doing a great job, and he is very proud of himself.

I love you very much,

Mom

LOVING YOU MORE EACH DAY

My Son,

Don't forget to pray.

I love you, thank you so much for your letters. How are you today?

I have been so very busy. I feel very guilty writing just a note, so I have to wait until I have a moment to think.

Finally, I am in Washington for a few weeks. The grass has grown and covered the doors. I left the house unattended; I was so tired from caring for mom when I left. I simply threw my hands into the air, locked the doors, and just left. I was away for 4 months in a row. I had never done that before . . . with everything in a total mess. That was it.

I am trying to do all I can in a short span of time because I have to pick mom up and bring her to Washington to see her friends.

I've tried to find someone to take the drive with me, because it will be a turnaround trip. I don't see so well when I drive in the evenings.

I am saving the cards and letters sent to me from the many well-wishing people. Some you know and many you don't know. These notes have restored my faith in humanity.

I pray all the time for your safe return, and I know God answers all prayers. In God's own time.

Be sure to rest. That's when God can recharge your battery, just as you charge your cell phone.

Jesse, this is a very difficult time for people. The American people are surrounded by so much violence. And we ask why our children are killing each other. I reply, "Why not? Everyone else is doing it." Everything today is upside down.

Anytime you can become a star without talent . . . by making a sex video the likes of Paris Hilton and the Kardashians . . .

Now, there is a Blk girl from Hip hop of Atlanta who has made a tape.

I am so embarrassed for the children of this generation.

Frederick Douglas said, "It is easier to raise strong children than to repair broken men."[1] With these role models, the children of our nation are in deep trouble.

A writer whose name I cannot remember said, "If you want to know the character of a nation you must look at the values of its women and children."

I can't forget your judge. I, too, ask the question, "Why are we here?" Whenever I hear complaints or excuses, I ask this question. It is the most profound question for me at this time in my life; and I ask this question of my country.

I Love You With All That Is Within

LOVING YOU

My Son,

Don't forget to pray.

Sandi called me two nights ago. It was a pleasant surprise. She wanted to come over, but it was a little late for me and I was very tired. She said she would be on her way to see you the following day with little Jesse.

I hope your visit was wonderful.

I have been quite ill. It came to my attention that my mom became ill last year, January 14, 2013, and I became ill about the same time—amazing.

I am much better now. I have about 4 letters I have started and didn't finish. I will finish them soon.

Did you receive the books I sent?

I love you my son,

Mom

LOVING YOU ALWAYS

My Son,

Election night.

Read Paul.

I have written you two letters and misplaced them. When I find them, I will send them to you.

I love and miss you.

Had a great visit. Hold tight.

God is Good,

Mom

LOVING YOU

Dear Son,

Don't forget to pray.

I know you are fascinated w/ T. J., but don't forget about Paul.

I will have to return to school in order to assemble the sentences that truly express the joy I feel when I see you.

This is just a short note to let you know I love you dearly, and we have returned safely.

I am now on my way to Fort Belvoir to pick up Mom's medicine. Of course, she found the base farthest from me to receive her care. But that's my mother. She was glad to know you looked well.

Jesse, you must remember Everything is in Divine Order. God is in on this, and that brings me great joy. I can assure you things will be alright.

God bless you and all around you,

Mom

Afterword

My mother, through her letters, sustained me through my darkest hour. She reminded me of the power of love, the power of mercy, and the power of forgiveness.

She helped correct my path, and put me on the road to redemption.

She saved me. By saving one person, she taught me that the nation could be saved as well.

With the highest honor and respect, thank you, Mom—from a grateful son.

Congressman Jesse L. Jackson, Jr.

Notes

November 5, 2013
1. Psalm 27:13 (KJV).

November 13, 2013
1. Psalm 23:2 (KJV).

November 23, 2013
1. John 10:10 (KJV).
2. Matthew 7:12 (KJV).

December 12, 2013
1. Luke 6:31 (KJV).

December 13, 2013
1. *Gone with the Wind.* Dir. Victor Fleming, George Cuker. Per. Clark Gable, Vivien Leigh, Thomas Mitchel (Metro-Goldwyn-Mayer, 1939), DVD.

December 21, 2013
1. Kirby Page, *Living Courageously* (New York: Farrar and Rhinehart, 1936).
2. Woodrow Wilson, *The New Freedom: A Call for the Emancipation of the Generous Energies of a People* (New York: Gray Rabbit Publications, 2011), 40.

January 5, 2014

1. *Forrest Gump*. Dir. Robert Zemeckis. Per. Tom Hanks, Sally Field, Mykelti Williamson, Robin Wright (Paramount Pictures, 1994), DVD.

January 12, 2014

1. Richard Lovelace, "To Althea, From Prison." *Stone Walls Do Not a Prison Make* (London: Unit Library, Ltd, 1904), Kindle Edition.

June 6, 2014

1. Philippians 4:11 (KJV).

November 3, 2014

1. Philippians 4:11 (KJV).

December 15, 2014

1. Eric Metaxes, *Miracles: What Are They, Why They Happen, and How They Can Change Your Life* (New York: Penguin Random House, 2015), Kindle Edition.

January 30, 2015

1. Proverbs 23:7 (KJV) February 24, 2015.

February 24, 2015

1. Eleanor Roosevelt, *You Learn by Living: Eleven Keys for a More Fulfilling Life* (New York: Harper Perennial, 2011), 29.

August 1, 2015

1. Robert Wingate, *East Meets West: Quotes of Wisdom and Inspiration*, Lulu.com, 45.

2. Oscar Wilde, *The Importance of Being Earnest* (New York: Dover Publications, 1990), 28.

Undated #13

1. Frederick Douglass quotes. BrainyQuote.com, Xplore Inc., 2018. https://www.brainyquote.com/quotes/frederick_douglass_201574, accessed May 13, 2018.